BEYOND THE BARRICADES

D0743719

Edited by Iris Tillman Hill and Alex Harris

Text research by Michael Kirkwood, Lesley Lawson, and Laura Mangan

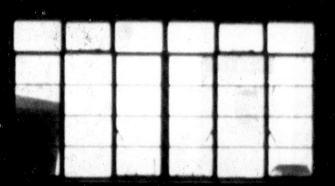

An Aperture Book in association with
the Center for Documentary Studies at Duke University

with the cooperation of Afrapix and
the Centre for Documentary Photography, Cape Town

BEYOND THE BARRICADES
POPULAR RESISTANCE IN SOUTH AFRICA

Photographs by twenty South African photographers

Photographs selected by Omar Badsha, Gideon Mendel, and Paul Weinberg

Historical essay by André Odendaal

Foreword by the Reverend Frank Chikane

Personal accounts collected from published sources, archives, lawyers' files, and court records

To all who continue to fight for freedom in our land.

Aperture Foundation, Inc. publishes a periodical, books, and portfolios of fine photography to communicate with creative people and serious photographers everywhere. A complete catalog is available upon request. Address: 20 East 23 Street, New York, New York 10010.

The staff at Aperture for *Beyond the Barricades* is Michael E. Hoffman, Executive Director; Steve Dietz, Editor; Lisa Rosset, Managing Editor; Barbara Levine, Assistant Editor; Laura Allen, Editorial Work-Scholar; Stevan Baron, Production Director; Linda Tarack, Production Assistant.

The staff at the Center for Documentary Studies for *Beyond the Barricades* is Iris Tillman Hill, Executive Director; Alex Harris, Professor of the Practice of Documentary Studies; Margaret Sartor, Book Designer; Julia Harper Day, Program Coordinator.

About the Personal Accounts: *Beyond the Barricades* includes statements by South Africans who were detained by the police or were subjected to attacks by vigilantes or the security forces. Some of these statements exist as court records or can be found in lawyers' files. Many have been provided for this book by human rights and legal organizations in South Africa. Other materials have been gathered from archives and published sources including newspapers, magazines, and books. The personal accounts appear in sections throughout the book as verbal portraits accompanying the photographs.

Editors' Note: In South Africa the term "black" is used to denote all people who are not caucasian. The apartheid system divides people into racial classifications such as Coloured, African, Indian, and Asian. In this book, in describing and documenting the political landscape in South Africa, it has been necessary to use the very classifications the South African government has imposed on its people.

Book design by Margaret Sartor

Library of Congress Catalog Number 88-82887
ISBN 0-89381-375-3

This book is published in conjunction with traveling exhibitions in southern Africa, the United States, Japan, Germany, England, France, and Holland. The exhibition, *South Africa under Apartheid,* will open at the United Nations in March 1990.

CONTENTS

Today

Everyone who has died
Is here today
Those who died in the struggle of the people
Are here
Singing with us—
They are holding our hands,
Just that touch
Moving through all our bodies
Like a bloodstream.

Biko
Is here today
Neil Agget
Who died for the liberation of workers
Is here today
Ephraim Shabalala
Who died
The system's victim
Is here today
Andries Raditsela
Who died
For us all
Is here today,
With us
Sharing,
This day with us.

Those who died as oppressors are here—
They weep about their past
Their hands are swollen

They cannot hold our hands
I can feel their cold breath
Brushing my shoulders.

Our babies and children who died
Because of the system
Are here playing around
On this day
They are observing and learning
From us for their next lives.

Our brothers and sisters,
Mothers and fathers
Who died confused,
Without making up their minds
Are here today
They want to put their arms around us and sing:
"Hlanganani Basebenzi"

The oppressors, the killers,
The murderers, assassins,
The traitors, the impimpis
All those who were against our people's freedom
—Are wandering among us
They are looking closely
Into our eyes
They want to speak
To us about what they have done
But there is no way for us
To be aware of their presence.

Away oppressor
Away traitor
Go away
Go away,
All those who were against peace and justice,
Must go away from us today.
Today!

Nise Malange

6

PREFACE

This collection of photographs depicts one of the longest and bloodiest periods of political resistance to apartheid, a time of mass mobilization and brutal repression.

Where did we as photographers find ourselves in this turbulent landscape? We witnessed intimately the struggle around us, both the euphoria as the popular movement gained momentum, and the tragedy as the state responded violently to this challenge.

Photography took on a particular significance in this period of our history as it provided irrefutable documentation of popular resistance and state brutality. The "camera" became a voice for those denied a vote and basic human rights, and was instrumental in bringing the South African struggle to the international arena.

The state responded by focusing its attack on the media. The camera was accused of being an instrument of insurrection. When the State of Emergency was redeclared in June 1986, the already existing restrictions were made even more extensive.

4.(1) No person shall without the prior consent of the Commissioner or of a member of a security force serving as a commissioned officer in that force take any photograph or make or produce any television recording, film recording, drawing or other depiction—(a) of any unrest or security action or of any incident occurring in the course thereof, including the damaging or destruction of property or the injuring or killing of persons, or (b) of any damaged or destroyed property or injured or dead persons or other visible signs of violence at the scene where unrest or security action is taking place or has taken place or of any injuries sustained by any person in or during unrest or security action (from the Government Gazette of the Republic of South Africa, Vol. 276, no. 11342).

Many of the photographs included in this book could not be taken today.

In 1988, the South African government went further, imposing severe restrictions on eighteen political, trade-union, youth, and civic organizations. This was another attempt to destroy the mass-based popular movement whose growth is documented here. The restrictions came eleven years after the Nationalist government used similar measures to smash the black consciousness movement and twenty-eight years after the banning of the African National Congress and Pan Africanist Congress. It has become clear that the periods between these waves of mass uprisings are becoming progressively shorter and the state's response more violent with every cycle. These photographs are one part of the collective memory that stands against the apartheid government's efforts to blot out our history.

The historical significance of this period of resistance is that both activists and ordinary people began to look beyond the barricades of apartheid toward a new South Africa. As communities were debating and discussing the shape of a future post-apartheid society, photographers were drawn into this process and began to question the traditional practice of photography. This collective document and accompanying exhibition represent an approach to documentary photography among a growing number of both black and white South African photographers. Since the early 1980s, these photographers have been coming together to share their skills, ideas, and work as part of a commitment to documentary photography and nonracialism.

All the photographers represented in this book have experienced state repression. Some have been beaten up by the security forces, and others detained without trial. All have had their film confiscated and been denied the possibility of photographing in conflict situations.

The camera has played a special role in these times. It has been there to record inhumanity, injustice, and exploitation. It searches for peace and hope. It is beckoned by history to take sides. The photographers in this book have.

The Photographers

FOREWORD

I Am a Living Witness

Beyond the Barricades is the latest and clearest account by South Africans of resistance to apartheid within their own country. It also provides an analysis of the South African government's counter-strategies, what the apartheid regime calls its "total strategy" against the "total onslaught" of those who oppose it. The book describes the events that led to a crisis in the white domination of South Africa, and it tells of the related loss of ideological control of the black majority. The government's decision to impose a new constitution in the name of reform without including black participation mobilized the democratic resistance in South Africa. By excluding the African majority from the tricameral Parliament, the government forced all democratic groups in the country and particularly the black majority to join in resisting its implementation. The democratic forces understood that this new constitutional structure was simply another way of entrenching apartheid and racist supremacist ideology in South Africa.

After the heavily boycotted tricameral parliamentary elections in August 1984, people in the black townships refused to cooperate with the apartheid government. They refused to collaborate with the system in their own oppression. They refused to be governed by the apartheid regime against their will. To assume responsibility for their own lives, they formed local grass-roots organizations including street committees, defense committees, people's education committees, and even people's courts. This creation of independent community governments run by local people led to a serious crisis for the government. The government resorted to a repressive state apparatus to disrupt and destroy these local efforts. The government, on the one hand, used "reform" in its strategy to disarm the democratic opposition. Reform measures were part of the carrot-and-stick strategy to win the hearts and minds of our people and to co-opt them into the system while eliminating all forms of opposition to this system.

What followed, as André Odendaal makes clear in his accompanying text, was a "chronicle of terror" that is dramatically encapsulated by the story of the twenty-one-year-old Caiphus Nyoka who was assassinated at his home in 1987. This state-sponsored chronicle of terror included the declaration of a state of emergency, mass detentions, political assassinations by murder death squads, and brutal acts by security forces (South African Defense Force and the police), particularly against children under ten years old. It involved vigilante attacks against anti-apartheid groups and leaders. In some cases, these vigilantes were apparently supported by South African security forces.

The period covered by this book represents a period of untold brutality, misery, suffering, pain, and even death. The photographs and text tabulate and bring to life the extent of this misery. Endless funerals and victims of attacks are portrayed. The reader experiences the full impact of the state's increased militarization and its brutal response to the people's determination that change must come. Historic moments of courage by women, youth workers, and leaders unfold in these pages. Graphic inci-

dents that became almost a daily story, gathered together in this book, convey the full horror and intensity of the sacrifice and courage of the oppressed people of South Africa. The pictures convey more powerfully than words ever could the grief and yet the determination of such people. Because of such pictures, the truth can be conveyed and remembered long after the tears have dried and the people have passed on.

I personally am a living witness to this chronicle of resistance portrayed in *Beyond the Barricades*. I was part of the leadership of the United Democratic Front (UDF) in 1984 and 1985 who were detained and charged with high treason and later acquitted. Brothers and sisters, mothers and fathers, friends and compatriots have died, disappeared, or been removed from our midst, kept for long periods in the dungeons of apartheid prisons.

Even as this book goes to press, the war has not ended. Instead, it has intensified, with many still in detention. Some have entered their third year of imprisonment without being charged with any crime. Almost all the major organizations that used nonviolence and peaceful means of change are effectively banned or restricted, and some of those who played a leadership role are also restricted, while many have gone underground or have left the country.

In the midst of this misery, I have had to make sense of my faith in a God of justice, mercy, and love. This was not always easy, especially when, while in detention, a deacon of the white church of my faith was supervising my torture! What I have realized, however, is that my faith was what kept me alive, and that when one's faith is that of a fundamental, living belief in overcoming injustice, it becomes a very dangerous and threatening weapon in the eyes of the South African government.

There are various dilemmas for me in the context of my faith in the struggle. One is as a pastor to young people who increasingly are battered by the system and see no *alternative* to violence, as the only means of change. This is the crisis that we all face at present in this country in light of the ever-increasing dehumanization and brutality of the South African regime.

The regime's strategy of constitutional reforms is in a serious crisis. Political strategies have almost all collapsed. The only way this regime continues to remain in power is through brute force and violence against the black majority. It has by now almost resorted to a 100 percent military operation and solution as opposed to peaceful and political solutions.

This book will help the reader to develop an understanding of the complex situation and crisis we are facing in South Africa, and it will also help those who are directly involved in the action against the apartheid regime to understand better how they can become more effective.

The Reverend Frank Chikane
General Secretary, South African Council of Churches

THE PHOTOGRAPHERS

Omar Badsha
Julian Cobbing
Paul Grendon
Dave Hartman
Steve Hilton-Barber
Rashid Lombard
Roger Meintjies
Gideon Mendel
Eric Miller
Santu Mofokeng
Themba Nkosi
Cedric Nunn
Billy Paddock
Myron Peters
Chris Qwazi
Jeeva Rājgopaul
Guy Tillim
Zubeida Vallie
Gill de Vlieg
Paul Weinberg

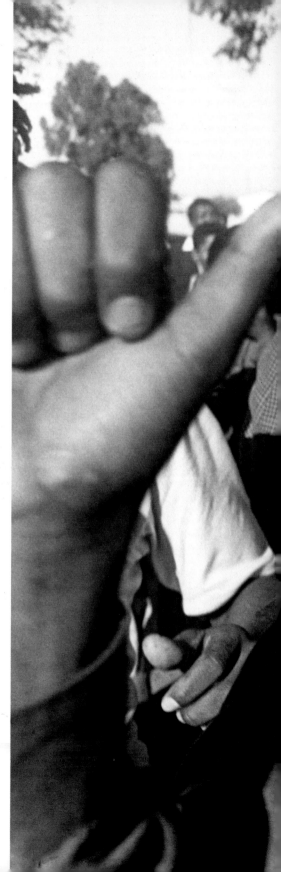

Preceding page, a pall bearer presses on through tear gas at the funeral of one of 50 people killed by ''Witdoeke'' vigilantes, Crossroads, Cape Town, May 1986.

Opposite, P. W. Botha takes the salute at a military parade in Pretoria, November 1980. Before he became state president of South Africa in 1983, Botha headed the Ministry of Defense and later became prime minister in 1978. He is shown here with his close supporter General Magnus Malan, minister of Defense, on his left. During Botha's presidency, South Africa has been transformed into an increasingly militarized ''emergency state,'' under siege from elements both within and outside the country. General Malan is widely regarded as the most influential member of South Africa's powerful National Security Council.

Above, children and other spectators look on as members of the 101 Battalion, recruited in Namibia, drill at a parade in Cape Town in 1987, celebrating the seventy-fifth year of the South African Defense Force. Military parades in South Africa are intended to boost propaganda claims that the military can win the support of black South Africans without granting them any rights of citizenship. Although blacks who enlist in the South African Defense Force face ostracism in their communities, many join the army out of desperate economic necessity. There have been numerous alleged incidents in which some members of the 101 Battalion have doubled in their ''off-duty'' hours as violence-prone, right-wing vigilantes, attacking other blacks who have been active in the political struggle against apartheid.

Freedom song

Those who are against us,
We shall reckon with them,
The day we take our land back—
Their names are written down.

When there's a roll call of our heroes,
I wonder if my name will be on that roll,
I wonder what it will be like
When we sit with Tambo
And tell him about the fall of the Boers.

Mrs. Elize Botha, wife of the state president, and Mrs. Tshabalala, wife of the mayor of Soweto, leave the town council building in August 1984 after President and Mrs. Botha were granted "the freedom of the township" in a ceremony derived from an old British tradition. In townships like Soweto, blacks, who are excluded from the new constitution, are allowed to vote for "community councils," which have a limited measure of authority at the local level. A majority of South Africans consider officers who serve in these municipal government units to be collaborators in the apartheid state. Numerous people also call for boycotts of elections. In townships where there is a high percentage of politically aware blacks, the elections have been heavily boycotted. In Soweto only five percent of those who registered to vote participated in the elections. The "five-percenters" who participate in the apartheid government's system tend to be well off, and Mr. Tshabalala, a millionaire, reaps profits from government contracts. Mr. and Mrs. Tshabalala may seem to have "rights," but this is an exception, not a true picture of political and economic conditions for most South African blacks.

KwaZulu homeland Chief Mangosuthu Gatsha Buthelezi, on the left, and Goodwill Zwelithini, the traditional king of the Zulus, appear at the ceremonial opening of the KwaZulu legislature in 1986. Buthelezi wields the political power as chief minister of the homeland, KwaZulu, established under the government's apartheid system, while King Goodwill sits on the throne as monarch in name only. In the traditional world of the Zulus, Buthelezi was a member of the royal household in a clan that served the king. In government-established KwaZulu, Buthelezi, once a vocal opponent of the government, now is considered an ally in the suppression of broad-based democratic organizations like the United Democratic Front (UDF) and the Congress of South African Trade Unions (COSATU). Buthelezi leads the Zulu nationalist organization Inkatha, whose members have been involved in violent conflicts with supporters of the UDF and COSATU. Because Buthelezi endorses significant aspects of the government system, he enjoys support from the state. There are many reports of police routinely looking the other way when members of Inkatha attack opponents of the government. The state-controlled media reports these conflicts as "black-on-black violence," which disguises the true nature of these political conflicts. They are in fact attempts to wipe out democratic opposition in the area.

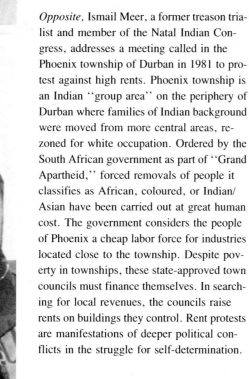

Opposite, Ismail Meer, a former treason trialist and member of the Natal Indian Congress, addresses a meeting called in the Phoenix township of Durban in 1981 to protest against high rents. Phoenix township is an Indian "group area" on the periphery of Durban where families of Indian background were moved from more central areas, rezoned for white occupation. Ordered by the South African government as part of "Grand Apartheid," forced removals of people it classifies as African, coloured, or Indian/Asian have been carried out at great human cost. The government considers the people of Phoenix a cheap labor force for industries located close to the township. Despite poverty in townships, these state-approved town councils must finance themselves. In searching for local revenues, the councils raise rents on buildings they control. Rent protests are manifestations of deeper political conflicts in the struggle for self-determination.

Above, residents of Newlands East township demonstrate against government-nominated town councilors in Durban, 1981. Because local councils have been imposed on the people of the townships by the National party-controlled government, the residents, for the most part, refuse to support them. The elaborately structured governing system, established to maintain apartheid, has been enormously expensive both to the South African government and to the people forced to live under this divisive system.

Opposite, Albertina Sisulu, a leader of the United Democratic Front, briefs a group of women before they embark on a National Women's Day picket in Johannesburg, August 1984. Women's Day commemorates a 1955 march by women protesting against the extension of the pass laws to women. On this day in 1984, members of the Federation of Transvaal Women (FEDTRAW) demonstrated for human rights in the center of the city. *On the left,* a woman protests conditions in rural areas where many blacks live. In these remote homelands, blacks often go hungry because they are unable to farm the poor, crowded land where they live, and there are few jobs for them to earn sufficient incomes to feed, clothe, and house their families. There is an enormous disparity of income in South Africa between the white and black population. *Above,* another woman from FEDTRAW carries a picket. Under State of Emergency regulations and the Riotous Assemblies Act popular protest is severely restricted. To demonstrate, one must have a magistrate's permission, which allows only limited picketing. Members of FEDTRAW have been charged with sedition and subversion and held in detention without trial as the government works to immobilize and disrupt opposition to apartheid.

Opposite, Frances Baard, a former president of the African National Congress's Women's League, salutes the crowd gathered to launch the United Democratic Front in Mitchell's Plain, Cape Town, August 1983. The UDF is the largest nonracial, popular movement for democracy, organized in opposition to the new constitution of 1983. Under this constitution, the government formed a tricameral parliament with three houses: the House of Assembly (white), the House of Representatives (coloured), and the House of Delegates (Indian), but designed the white House of Assembly so that it totally dominated the parliament and had all the power. The government denied Africans any representation, claiming they were represented in their tribal homelands. The UDF drew together over 600 democratically based community, student, trade union, women's, and church organizations and was the major legal oppositional force until the government severely curtailed its activities in 1988. In 1987, both Albertina Sisulu and Francis Baard were leaders in organizing women in the UDF, which was seen as a successor to its historic counterpart, the banned African National Congress's Women's League. Political activists of the 1980s have deliberately defined links to earlier protest movements, like the ANC, insisting on the continuity of the democratic resistance in South Africa.

Left, Dorothy Nyembe, imprisoned for being a member of the banned ANC's military wing, *Umkhonto we Sizwe,* is welcomed home to KwaMashu township, Durban, 1984, after spending fifteen years in prison.

Now, we as mothers, what must we say? We say to you—we are sick and tired of what is happening. We see our children being sent to jail for nothing. We see people being sent to the borders—they are going to kill people.

Frances Baard

They Would Follow Her

Police harassment at meeting places and at homes is a problem. For example, a woman was active in organizing, and her house was watched every Saturday and Sunday morning. They would park their car right opposite her house for a few hours. Then they would follow her until she was at the meeting place. On the day of a meeting people are intercepted and asked where they are going and why they are going there.

Some people used to besmirch the organizer's character, and discourage us from associating with her. Anonymous threatening letters are often sent to active members. Ministers of religion are also intimidated not to allow meetings at their churches. Some churches take the struggle from the people and believe that God will provide.

Women are threatened with detention and are made to fear for their children's lives if it happens.

from *South African Women Speak*

The Children Suffer the Most

Today—although the people are struggling, there is too much pressure from the government. Too many people are being killed.

In the 1950s the police were seen more as men of the law. Today to see a policeman is to see a gun pointing at you.

We are working for action, but also unity. So that if there is an issue we all think is important, women from all points of view will come together.

The most important issues for women to organize around and educate themselves about today are mass removals, passes, influx control, the cost of living. The people experiencing mass removals suffer the most and the children suffer the most.

These children are taken from a six-roomed house and dumped in a single corrugated-iron room. Children of 15 years cannot sleep in the same room with their parents. And the children are dying. Look at Thornhill where the children died like flies.

Albertina Sisulu
from *South African Women Speak*

We Are Sick and Tired

Let's forget for a minute we are women. Let's say we are the mothers. We are mothers—we see what is taking place in this country. A mother will hold the knife on the sharp end. Today we see our people being sent to jail every day—there are detentions, the courts are crowded every day, people in exile, people rotting in jails.

Now, we as mothers, what must we say? We say to you—we are sick and tired of what is happening. We see our children being sent to jail for nothing. We see people being sent to the borders—they are going to kill people.

As mothers we endorse what others have been saying. A national convention must be called so that our leaders must come and solve the problem which is confronting our country. We've got people in exile—we tell the government we want those leaders to come home. We have got people who are rotting in the jails—we say we want those people to come home.

Frances Baard
from *South African Women Speak*

We Decided to Burn our Passes

Last year people from all over South Africa went to Cradock, a small town, far away in the Great Karoo. They went to the funeral of UDF leader Mathew Goniwe and his three comrades.

There was an old woman at the funeral. She wore a long black dress with Goniwe's picture pinned to her back. Her ankles were swollen so it was hard for her to walk. This woman is Mrs. Nonyanga Sibanda.

Everyone in Cradock knows Mrs. Sibanda. People call her "The General" because Mrs. Sibanda is a brave fighter. Mrs. Sibanda has fought against the government for most of her life:

Cradock has never been quiet. You know Canon Calata, the first general secretary of the ANC, came from Cradock. So everyone in Cradock knew the ANC right from the beginning.

I was a member of the ANC Women's League. I remember our first big fight well. It was at the time of the Defiance Campaign when people all over South Africa broke the apartheid laws.

In Cradock we decided to burn our passes. So, one day we went from house to house, collecting everyone's passes. But we also collected knives because the men often stabbed each other at the beerhalls. We wanted to stop this too.

The next day the police came—on horseback. They carried big sticks. They arrested more than fifty men and women. I was one of them. But it wasn't only people in Cradock who were arrested. People were arrested everywhere and the jails were full. We went to a jail on the Fish River. They kept me there for eighteen months. The police said I was one of the troublemakers. In the end I went to court. They sentenced me to eight more months in jail.

When the ANC was banned in 1960, Mrs. Sibanda was arrested again. Mrs. Sibanda was charged with treason, together with four other women from Cradock. The judge said they were guilty. So Mrs. Sibanda spent the next three years in jail. When she came out, she was banned for five years:

People in Cradock carried on fighting, but they did not organize well. When the leaders were arrested, that was it. No one did anything. They waited for the leaders to come out of jail.

But in 1983 things started to change. The UDF came to Cradock—mainly because of Mathew Goniwe. People started to organize. The youth started Cradoya—the Cradock Youth Association. The people in Lingelihle started

Cradora—the Cradock Residents Association, and the women started Crawo—the Cradock Women's Organization.

Mrs. Sibanda is the deputy president of Cradora, the residents' association. They have started committees on every street. Even the police say that Lingelihle is well organized. They say all 24,000 people in Lingelihle would hear a message in half an hour—even when meetings were banned.

from *Learn and Teach* Magazine

The Houses are Cracked and Broken

The women's group in Lamontville was formed in November 1983. Nobody knew where to get help. There was fighting after Mr. Dube had been killed. Many police came in with tear gas. It went on day and night. Police camped up in the hills by the clinic the whole month until July. People could not be on the streets at night. The police would come into the houses kicking the doors down and hitting people with sjamboks [plastic whips]. The police tried to make the girls love them. Then there was the rent increase and the bus boycott as well.

We women spoke about the problems. Children with no place to stay, no food, no work. At first 15 women joined the group. Each paid 50¢ a month. Now we meet at the church every week. A lot of women are finding it difficult to make meetings at night, six o'clock, because they have to cook for children and husbands. Some men do not like their wives to come out. We are talking about changing our meetings to a Saturday and Sunday instead of a weekday so that more women would be free to come. But women have carried on joining—we have grown to 100. We are a branch of the Natal Organization of Women. We hope that there will be branches all over Natal.

In March we went to see the superintendent of Lamontville, Mr. Turner, of the Port Natal Administration Board. He was prepared to close doors on people who had no money to pay rent. We organized as women because we thought we would be safe from tear gas and shooting. We could appeal on behalf of our children. We wrote a letter to take with us.

When we came to Port Natal Administration Board the policeman at the gate said, "You're not allowed to see the superintendent." We told him, "You're not allowed to stop us at the gate." So he let us in. At the Administration Board office we saw policemen gathering around with their guns. This did not worry us—nothing happened. We asked Mr. Turner why the rents are going up when the houses are cracked and broken. They should speak to the people first and ask them why they are not paying rent before closing houses and taking furniture.

Mr. Turner said he would take our complaints to Mayville [suburb of Durban]. We knew he did not take our letter there. Instead, he took it to Mr. Nxasane who is a councilor. He said we must talk to the councilors and not him. There is no point in going to the councilors. They do nothing for the people. Nothing has been done about the letter.

from *South African Women Speak*

We Want All Our Rights

I believe we are standing at the birth of what could become the greatest and most significant people's movement in more than a quarter of a century. We are here to say that the government's constitutional proposals are inadequate, that they do not express the will of the vast majority of South Africa's people. More than that, we are here to say that what we are working for is one undivided South Africa which shall belong to all of its people.

The time has come for white people in this country to realize that their destiny is inextricably bound with our destiny, that they shall never be free until we are free. People who think that their security and peace lie in the perpetration of intimidation, dehumanization and violence are not free. They will never be free as long as they have to kill our children in order to safeguard their overprivileged positions. They will never be free as long as they have to lie awake at night worrying whether a black government will one day do to them as they are doing to us, when white power will have come to its inevitable end.

To be sure, the new proposals will make apartheid less blatant in some ways. It will be modernized and streamlined, and in its new multicoloured cloak, it will be less conspicuous and less offensive to some. Nonetheless, it will still be there. And we must remember, apartheid is a thoroughly evil system and as such it cannot be modified, modernized or streamlined. It has to be irrevocably eradicated.

Let me remind you of three little words, words that express so eloquently our seriousness in this struggle. You don't have to have a vast vocabulary to understand them. You don't need a philosophical bent to grasp them. They are just three little words. The first word is "all." We want all our rights, not just a few token handouts the government sees fit to give—we want all *our rights. And we want all of South Africa's people to have their rights. Not just a selected few, not just "Coloureds" or "Indians," after they have been made honorary whites. We want the rights of all South Africans [to be restored to them], including those whose citizenship has already been stripped away by this government.*

The second word is "here." We want all our rights here *in a united, undivided South Africa. We do not want them in impoverished homelands, we don't want them in our separate little group areas. We want them in this land which one day we shall once again call our own.*

The third word is "now." We want all our rights, we want them here, and we want them now. We have been waiting so long, we have been struggling so long. We have pleaded, cried, petitioned too long now. We have been jailed, exiled, killed for too long. Now is the time.

The Reverend Allan Boesak
from *South Africa: A Different Kind of War*

United Democratic Front president, Archie Gumede (center), leads the singing at the UDF's first public meeting in Natal Province, at Pietermaritzburg, October, 1983. The UDF successfully organized a massive boycott against the elections for the tricameral parliament. On the day before the rally five students were killed and over 100 injured when Inkatha *impis* (tribal army), protected by KwaZulu police, attacked the University of Zululand campus after students protested against Chief Buthelezi. This conflict was the turning point in the relationship between Chief Buthelezi and the non-racial movement (UDF), and the beginning of blood-letting in Natal.

Top left, Archie Gumede, president of the United Democratic Front, negotiates with police to allow family and friends to attend the 1985 Pietermaritzburg treason trial. Gumede, along with other UDF leaders, took refuge in the British consulate in Durban when the government began arresting UDF activists. They remained in the consulate for three months, creating an international diplomatic crisis, until they agreed to emerge. The South African state promptly charged them with "high treason," and they were put on trial in Pietermaritzburg. However, the government's case collapsed, and Gumede and the others were acquitted and released. Gumede was a defendant in what is known as the "original" Treason Trial of 1956–1960 when 156 leaders of the Congress Alliance were charged with treason. The Congress Alliance was an alliance of democratic organizations, including the ANC, SA Indian Congress, the Coloured Peoples Congress, and the Congress of Democrats. In June 1955 it convened the Congress of the People during which the Freedom Charter was adopted. The Freedom Charter was used by the state as one of the charges against the 156. The Treason Trial lasted five years and ended in acquittal of all the accused.

Center left, in 1984, Billy Nair left Durban Prison at the end of a twenty-year sentence for his activity in the African National Congress. Like Nelson Mandela, Nair spent many years on Robben Island where the state incarcerates thousands of political prisoners. A year after his release, in 1985, Nair was back in prison again, among thousands of others who had been detained without trial under the State of Emergency regulations. While in detention, Nair charged that he was tortured by police officers (a routine occurrence for political detainees) and suffered eye and ear injuries. After this incident, Nair and other UDF leaders went into hiding.

Bottom left, Mahammed Valli, Transvaal secretary of the United Democratic Front, and other spectators peer into the courtroom at the start of the Delmas treason trial. There were originally twenty-two UDF and other activists charged with furthering the aims of the African National Congress and with conspiring to overthrow the government of the state. One focus of the case was antirent protests in townships in the Vaal Triangle in 1984 that set in motion a continuous wave of civil unrest. The Delmas trial began on October 16, 1985, was moved to Pretoria on August 1, 1987, and ended in December 1988 after 446 days, which makes it the longest political trial in South African history. The trial was marked by repeated bail applications in an effort to get the defendants out of detention. Of the 22 accused, three were acquitted when the state concluded its case in 1986. In 1987 the accused offered their evidence, and in 1988 defense witnesses took the stand. "The trial in which 19 men faced charges of treason, subversion, murder, terrorism, and furthering the aims of the African National Congress and the South African Communist party [was] of tremendous political significance, involving as it [did], key figures of the now-restricted United Democratic Front" (*Weekly Mail,* June 24, 1988). In Pretoria, it was heard in Criminal Court C, the same courtroom in which Nelson Mandela and his codefendants received their life sentences in the Rivonia trial of 1964.

Professor Ismail Mohamed, a United Democratic Front leader, reaches out to his daughter Elaine as he is arrested by South African security police. Mohamed was detained and charged with treason along with fifteen others in the Pietermaritzburg treason trial in Johannesburg, February 1985. Eventually, all were exonerated. Reacting to the increasing strength of the UDF and its successful elections' boycott, the state brought charges against many UDF leaders, alleging treason, subversion, and related offenses. In many cases, proceedings dragged on for years, effectively immobilizing key opponents of the government, who remained in detention while awaiting trial.

FREEDOM CHARTER

Adopted by the Congress of the People, 26 June 1955

Preamble

We the people of South Africa, declare for all our country and the world to know:—

That South Africa belongs to all who live in it, black and white, and that no government can justly claim authority unless it is based on the will of the people;

That our people have been robbed of their birthright to land, liberty and peace by a form of government founded on injustice and inequality;

That our country will never be prosperous or free until all our people live in brotherhood, enjoying equal rights and opportunities;

That only a democratic state, based on the will of the people can secure to all their birthright without distinction of color, race, sex or belief;

And therefore, we, the people of South Africa, black and white, together—equals, countrymen and brothers—adopt this FREEDOM CHARTER. And we pledge ourselves to strive together, sparing nothing of our strength and courage, until the democratic changes here set out have been won.

The People Shall Govern!

Every man and woman shall have the right to vote for and stand as a candidate for all bodies which make laws.

All the people shall be entitled to take part in the administration of the country.

The rights of the people shall be the same regardless of race, color or sex.

All bodies of minority rule, advisory boards, councils and authorities shall be replaced by democratic organs of self-government.

All National Groups Shall Have Equal Rights!

There shall be equal status in the bodies of state, in the courts and in the schools for all national groups and races;

All national groups shall be protected by law against insults to their race and national pride;

All people shall have equal rights to use their own language and to develop their own folk culture and customs;

The preaching and practice of national, race or color discrimination and contempt shall be a punishable crime;

All apartheid laws and practices shall be set aside.

The People Shall Share in the Country's Wealth!

The national wealth of our country, the heritage of all South Africans, shall be restored to the people;

The mineral wealth beneath the soil, the banks and monopoly industry shall be transferred to the ownership of the people as a whole;

All other industries and trade shall be controlled to assist the well-being of the people;

All people shall have equal rights to trade where they choose, to manufacture and to enter all trades, crafts and professions.

The Land Shall Be Shared Among Those Who Work It!

Restriction of land ownership on a racial basis shall be ended, and all the land redivided amongst those who work it, to banish famine and land hunger;

The state shall help the peasants with implements, seed, tractors and dams to save the soil and assist the tillers;

Freedom of movement shall be guaranteed to all who work on the land;

All shall have the right to occupy land wherever they choose;

People shall not be robbed of their cattle, and forced labor and farm prisons shall be abolished.

All Shall Be Equal Before the Law!

No one shall be imprisoned, deported or restricted without a fair trial;

No one shall be condemned by the order of any Government official;

The courts shall be representative of all the people;

Imprisonment shall be only for serious crimes against the people, and shall aim at reeducation, not vengeance;

The police force and army shall be open to all on an equal basis and shall be the helpers and protectors of the people;

All laws which discriminate on grounds of race, color or belief shall be repealed.

All Shall Enjoy Equal Human Rights!

The law shall guarantee to all their right to speak, to organize, to meet together, to publish, to preach, to worship and to educate their children;

The privacy of the house from police raids shall be protected by law;

All shall be free to travel without restriction from countryside to town, from province to province, and from South Africa abroad;

Pass laws, permits and all other laws restricting these freedoms shall be abolished.

There Shall Be Work and Security!

All who work shall be free to form trade unions, to elect their officers and to make wage agreements with their employers;

The state shall recognize the right and duty of all to work, and to draw full unemployment benefits;

Men and women of all races shall receive equal pay for equal work;

There shall be a forty-hour working week, a national minimum wage, paid annual leave, and sick leave for all workers, and maternity leave on full pay for all working mothers;

Miners, domestic workers, farm workers and civil servants shall have the same rights as all others who work;

Child labor, compound labor, the tot system and contract labor shall be abolished.

The Doors of Learning and of Culture Shall Be Opened!

The government shall discover, develop and encourage national talent for the advancement of our cultural life;

All the cultural treasures of mankind shall be open to all, by free exchange of books, ideas and contact with other lands;

The aim of education shall be to teach the youth to love their people and their culture, to honor human brotherhood, liberty and peace;

Education shall be free, compulsory, universal and equal for all children;

Higher education and technical training shall be opened to all by means of state allowances and scholarships awarded on the basis of merit;

Adult literacy shall be ended by a mass state education plan;

Teachers shall have all the rights of other citizens;

The color bar in cultural life, in sport and in education shall be abolished.

There Shall Be Houses, Security and Comfort!

All people shall have the right to live where they choose, to be decently housed, and to bring up their families in comfort and security;

Unused housing space to be made available to the people;

Rent and prices shall be lowered, food plentiful and no one shall go hungry;

A preventive health scheme shall be run by the state;

Free medical care and hospitalization shall be provided for all, with special care for mothers and young children;

Slums shall be demolished, and new suburbs built where all have transport, roads, lighting, playing fields, crèches [day-care centers] and social centers;

The aged, the orphans, the disabled and the sick shall be cared for by the state;

Rest, leisure and recreation shall be the right of all;

Fenced locations and ghettoes shall be abolished, and laws which break up families shall be repealed.

There Shall Be Peace and Friendship!

South Africa shall be a fully independent state, which respects the rights and sovereignty of all nations;

South Africa shall strive to maintain world peace and the settlement of all international disputes by negotiation—not war;

Peace and friendship amongst all our people shall be secured by upholding the equal rights, opportunities and status of all;

The people of the protectorates—Basutoland, Bechuanaland and Swaziland—shall be free to decide for themselves their own future;

The right of all the peoples of Africa to independence and self-government shall be recognized, and shall be the basis of close cooperation.

Let all who love their people and their country now say, as we say here:

"THESE FREEDOMS WE WILL FIGHT FOR, SIDE BY SIDE, THROUGHOUT OUR LIVES, UNTIL WE HAVE WON OUR LIBERTY."

A meeting called by the Natal Indian Congress, founded by Mahatma Gandhi at the turn of the century, protests against the planned imposition of the racially segregated tricameral parliament in 1984 in Chatsworth township. Despite conflicts with Inkatha, the United Democratic Front enjoyed strong support in Natal. In the boycotted election, only a small percentage of the few registered Indian voters went to the polls. Indian House of Delegates' politics is dominated by a long-standing personal feud between two wealthy leaders, whose political machines have controlled Indian apartheid politics for many years. The majority of Indians consider the House of Delegates a standing joke.

On election day, August 1984, the effect of the elections boycott is apparent in this picture of a policeman in a polling station in Overport township, Durban. The newspaper headline reads, ''Police Wade into Demonstrating Mob,'' while inside the polling stations the pace was much less hectic. There were many peaceful and orderly demonstrations against the elections throughout the country, and the success of the boycott reflected growing support for the United Democratic Front. Indeed, low as the polls were, the turnout depended upon massive efforts by the state-owned and government-supported media.

Police attack youths early in the morning on the day of the Pollsmoor Prison March. United Democratic Front leaders had called on people to march to Pollsmoor Prison in August 1985 to demand the release of Nelson Mandela and other political prisoners.

The march marked the beginning of intense clashes between police and youths in Cape Town. While they were marching for Mandela and other prisoners, the students were also protesting against the state's education system, which offers blacks inferior education. Demanding local control of education,

these students were at the forefront of the drive for "people's education." The police responded by intervening vigorously and sometimes violently in schools where boycotts were in progress.

Tambo's voice is heard calling—
let the new men and women emerge
amidst this
Botha's voice is heard calling—
tear gas, rubber bullets, Hippos and Casspirs
mow down the children, women and men
while Reagan smiles
and Thatcher grins
let them,
the friendship presents they give the Boers
are death makers for us
let them be friends.

Mongane Serote
from *A Tough Tale*

Barricades are erected on Belgravia Road, Athlone township, Cape Town, September 1985. As violence spread through the townships, barricades were thrown up on the streets where young people battled with the police. Within two months, the death toll had risen, and many were injured. The mood of resistance was reflected in a chant heard in the streets: "All the mothers and the fathers, the brothers and the sisters, the grandmothers and the grandfathers, the dogs and the cats—they all have joined in the struggle."

Above, a prison official approaches the families of death-row prisoners Wellington Meilies and Moses Jantjies to inform them that the two men had been hanged earlier that morning, Pretoria, 1987. ''My blood will nourish the tree which will bear the fruits of freedom. Tell my people that I love them and that they must continue the struggle. Do not worry about me but about those who are suffering.'' Solomon Mahlangu left this message for his mother just before he was executed for treason in 1979. Ten other African National Congress members were executed between 1979 and 1983. In 1987, when Meilies and Jantjies were executed, thirty-two political prisoners remained on death row in Pretoria Central Prison. South Africa has the highest number of hangings in the world.

Opposite, workers leaving a May Day meeting find riot police at the entrance blocking their way on the steps of Khotso House in Johannesburg, May 1985. The Congress of South African Trade Unions (COSATU) had called for a work stoppage on May Day in which 1.5 million workers participated. Khotso House was a building owned by the South African Council of Churches and headquarters for many progressive organizations including the United Democratic Front. One early morning in August 1988 a massive explosion destroyed the building. A similar blast a year earlier leveled Cosatu House, a building owned by the labor federation, COSATU. In October 1988, Khanya House, headquarters of the Southern African Catholic Bishops' Conference, was also wrecked by a mysterious arson attack. Government investigators claim that they cannot solve these and numerous other crimes against anti-apartheid organizations.

AIMS AND OBJECTS OF WORKING CLASS ORGANISATIONS

Police, carrying *sjamboks* (traditionally, rhinoceros-hide whips, now often made of flexible plastic), arrest a student after breaking up protests that followed the assassination of United Democratic Front leader and human rights lawyer Victoria Mxenge in Durban, July 1985. Chaotic and violent events followed Mxenge's death, signaling the escalation of the confrontation between the UDF and Inkatha, the Zulu nationalist organization, in the Natal region. Throughout the townships of South Africa in the summer of 1985, revolt and protests spread, leading to the government's proclamation of a State of Emergency in thirty-six districts in the country. Martial law was imposed in these areas.

Leaders of the United Women's Organization are turned back from Parliament and arrested during a march to protest against the massacre in which the police killed twenty-two people in the eastern Cape township of Langa. The Langa shootings occurred on 21 March 1985 and were the first mass killings during the 1985 uprising, falling on the twenty-fifth anniversary of the Sharpeville massacre. At Sharpeville, police opened fire on anti-pass law demonstrators, killing sixty-nine people. In Langa, the crowd was marching in a funeral procession when police fired at them. In the judicial inquiry into the incident, the state finally admitted culpability and paid a fine of over half a million dollars in damages. Eyewitnesses maintained that the police shot innocent people without provocation.

Opposite, youths burn the car of an alleged police informer following the funeral of four victims killed in the ''grenade incident'' in Duduza township, Transvaal, July 1985. On the morning of 26 June 1985, a group of young activists were killed by defective or booby-trapped hand grenades. The grenades had been given to them by an *agent provocateur,* a member of the security force, posing as an African National Congress guerrilla. Feelings ran high during the funeral, and violence erupted. Conflict between the people and armed police spread from township to township in what had become a war.

Above, a student taunts a black policeman during a demonstration following the assassination of United Democratic Front leader Victoria Mxenge, in Durban, August 1, 1985. Three weeks before her death, Mxenge attended a funeral for four other UDF leaders who had been murdered in Cradock in the eastern Cape. She was buried next to her husband, Griffiths Mxenge, also a victim of assassination several years earlier. These deaths are usually attributed to ''death squads,'' mysterious assassins who are rarely found and who work in a covert, sophisticated manner, unlike the highly visible vigilante gangs. Since 1978 over 150 activists have been assassinated with no one found responsible for these murders.

My Mother

My mother could never carry me
while they used the warmth of her womb
to forge their hearts into hatred

My mother could never wean me
because they dried her out
until her tits were arid tufts of drought

My mother could never embrace me
while she kept house for them
held their children

My mother is
a boesman meid
a kaffir girl
a koelie aunty
who wears beads of sweat around her neck
and chains around her ankles

But, defrocked of dignity
my mother has broken free of the heirlooms
of oppression

These days she dresses in the fatigues of those
grown tired of serving evil gods

Now my mother is dressed to kill

Chris van Wyk

Mourners clash with police during a wake at
the home of three-year-old Mnita Ngubeni,
who was shot in the head by police, Atteridge-
ville township, Pretoria, September 1985.
Funerals have been the occasions of confrontations with police throughout this period of
protest and upheaval. Young people and
children have been on the cutting edge of the
uprisings and have taken the greatest risks.
Many children have been shot, and many detained for lengthy periods in prison.

. . . school children took to the street one day. there will never be another soweto, nor, south africa. there are many kinds of deaths, and soweto knows them all, south africa too, and southern africa. you cannot kill children like cattle and then hope that guns are a monopoly.

Mongane Serote
from *Time Has Run Out*

Youths flee after clashing with police following a funeral in Duduza township, Transvaal, May 1985. Black townships across South Africa came to resemble war zones, as battles raged with police and army units. By late 1985, the streets of Duduza township were marked by killings and burnings. Lacking weapons, black youths improvised defenses that included erecting head-high trip wires against patrolling open-top vehicles and digging "tank traps" during the night when armored vehicles were lured into ambushes. To deal with the crisis, township residents formed street committees, which became in effect alternative local governments.

We Are Becoming Dangerous

I am confident. I know things will change—the problem is the "how" part of it. But I don't see any form of peaceful change. We can debate and debate about violence and nonviolence, as Christians, but that kind of intellectualizing is not going to change the course of events here. The simple fact is that the war has started. And as long as South Africa refuses to talk to the ANC, then the ANC is going to continue fighting. And the more people rise up inside to say "We want our rights" and then the government suppresses them, the more they will resort to arms and the ANC will become a home for them.

I've tried to talk to these guys when I was detained—the very ones who were interrogating me. They tried to threaten me, to say, "You see how powerful South Africa is, you are wasting your time, your people will only die if they try to fight against the system." But I always argue that it doesn't depend on how powerful a system is—the people will organize themselves to be equally powerful and destroy the system. Once a man has reached the stage where he doesn't care any more, even for his own life, then he becomes dangerous. So we are becoming dangerous. And this, the oppressor doesn't even know. I think the most tragic aspect of the oppressor vis-à-vis the oppressed is that the oppressor never knows the true feelings of the oppressed. So one day, he'll get a surprise.

The Reverend Frank Chikane
from *South Africa: A Different Kind of War*

Why Are You Taking My Mother?

The one incident when the police took me away [that stands out was when] my daughter said, "Just tell me, why are you taking my mother? I would like to know." This captain said to her, "Look, your mother is doing very good work, very good advice work, but we need to question her on a few things and that's why we're taking her." Then she said, "If you say she's doing very good work now, how on earth . . . Why are you taking her away? Just explain to me. I don't trust you people." The guy could not handle this twelve-year-old. There were lots of other people there, and they felt embarrassed. Without me telling her anything she questioned him.

The little one is eight years old. He said to me when I came out, "Are you going to continue your political work?" So I asked him, "What do you think? What should I do?" That was all in the beginning, the first week of my release. So he told me, "No, I think you should continue with your fight. I think the UDF does good work, and because you're in the UDF you should not leave what you're busy with. We would support you. We would stand by you. We would fight with you."

They actually agree to what I do. We've got a very nice relationship. Whatever problems I encounter at the Advice Office I always go back because there is nobody else to talk to. So when we sit around the table, we actually discuss it with them. We always talk about it in their terms, about how they would perceive it as children. I would always explain to them. They respond very well to it. They're very interested. They would go to meetings. They would inquire about it.

The other day they have these Mandela stickers. So my eldest son, who's ten years, he went to school and he said to me that he's going to explain to the kids about Mandela and he's taken all these stickers and he's going to give it to the kids. So in their way they're also trying to do something.

They respond well, although they feel very insecure, because they're not sure when we're going to be taken away. They adore their father very much, and they're not sure when he's going to be taken away.

While my children are concerned, I think they've made up their minds that they would also continue in the same footsteps, that they don't see their role in any other way. They've seen the viciousness of the police. They've seen how the police killed children when they came from school. I trust what they would do would be correct, because of my upbringing. And Johnny's [her former husband] upbringing.

Shahida Issel
from Die Trojaanse Perd

There Were Many of Us in the Cell

I am 28 years old and was arrested in 1981 and 1982 because I do not have a pass to live in Cape Town. I was convicted in the commissioner's court.

The last time I went to prison my children were about four years old and two years old. Both times I was arrested my children accompanied me to jail. Both children were ill with vomiting and diarrhea. I was allowed to take them to the prison hospital but the nurse did not give them the right medicine.

There were many of us in the cell . . . about 30 or 40.

There were no benches, and we were each given a mat and two blankets for sleeping. We slept on the cold cement floor as there were no beds.

During the day we cleaned our cell and the rest of the prison. The children stayed with us all the time. I would tie the baby on my back, and the older one would just stand next to me.

We never went outside for the whole five weeks.

The warders confiscated the food I took with me to prison. I do not think friends were allowed to bring food or clothing. So we had no change of clothing, apart from one napkin for the baby which I had to give back when I left.

We were woken at 5 A.M. and had a short time to wash ourselves and the babies. There was hot water. We fastened blankets with a safety pin around us while we washed our clothes and waited for them to dry. We had to hang them on the windows of our cells or spread them over the mats on the floor to dry.

In the mornings we had mielie meal, skim milk, a little bread and black coffee with no sugar.

At lunchtime, we ate mielie rice, usually with a little meat. We had vegetables once a week and no fruit at all.

In the evenings, we had porridge, mielie meal, coffee and a slice of dry bread, although sometimes it was spread with fat.

I think the time in prison was hard for the children. The baby had bronchitis by the time I was released. We received far too little food, and if we asked for more food it was refused. We also needed more blankets.

from South African Women Speak

We Have Always Been Scared

We have always been scared that the police will kill us and dump our bodies somewhere and that no one would even know about it. We are still scared, but at least now someone will know and perhaps they will not get away with it.

They Just Started Beating Her

One day I came home late from work. It was 6:30 P.M. A taxi stopped near my house, and a woman got out. She was carrying a lot of parcels and as she passed my house, some "greenflies" [municipal policemen] stopped her. They just started beating her with sjamboks [traditionally, rhinoceros-hide whips, now often made of flexible plastic]. She cried to them: "What have I done? I have come from work." They gave no reply. The "greenflies" saw that I was watching this, and they told me to go into my house. The woman had dropped her parcels, and her groceries were lying all over the street. You just can't send your children to the shop after half past six anymore. It seems that is how they want to control the townships. They want the people off the streets.

from Now Everyone Is Afraid:
The Changing Face of Policing in South Africa

I Was Then Hit, Whipped, and Sjambokked

On Friday, 8th August, a teacher who was teaching us, Mrs. M., stood before the whole class of 48 and told the boys that we have been born on a farm. She told us that we were like rubbish. We were insulted by this, and several of us told her that she should not talk to us in that manner. She then told us that we were not showing her any respect and left the classroom.

She returned shortly thereafter with some police who I recognize as from the administration board. The teacher pointed out a classmate of mine, V.M., and said to the police that he is the main troublemaker and noisemaker in the class. Two of the administration board police went to him and lifted him out of his desk by his shoulders and pushed a gun into his back. He tried to explain to them his understanding of what was going on, but they merely beat him in front of the class. They did this by making him bend over a chair right in front of the class and hit him approximately 10 times with a plastic whip which is approximately 4'6" long. In hitting him, this whip was whipped across his buttocks, mainly, but also bent around his front, and we could see that it hit his private parts.

After they had hit him, they grabbed me and in the same manner took me to the front of the class where they made me lie on the desk and hit me about 12 times all over my body.

I then returned to my desk, and the police of the administration board took V.M. out of the classroom. They then returned to the classroom and in the same manner as they had hit me, hit another school friend of mine, S.M. We were then both taken to the staffroom at gunpoint by members of the South African Police.

When I arrived in the staffroom there were approximately six or seven policemen of the South African police in there. S.M. and I were separated, and I was taken into a sideroom where members of the South African Police proceeded to assault me. As I entered the room, I hesitated, and a policeman known to me as "Sochiva" pointed his rifle at me and forced me at gun point to lie down. I was then hit, whipped and sjambokked at least 40 times all over my body. My back and buttocks were badly marked and bleeding. They then told me to get up and warned me that they had not yet finished with me and would come back to get me. They then told me to go back to the classroom. I had been so badly hit that I could not walk properly.

When I returned to the classroom, I found that all 28 boys in the class had been hit in the same way, while three of us had received the additional treatment in the staffroom. The girls were not beaten.

This attack on us lasted from approximately 8 A.M. to 9 A.M. in the morning. The teacher thereafter tried to run a normal class day. Later during the day the police on several occasions entered the classroom and asked if anybody had complaints. They told us that if we did have complaints, they would come and see us again.

As a result of the above-mentioned events, I am particularly fearful of returning to school as I believe the police intend carrying out their continued threats to assault us. I want to continue my education, but in the circumstances find it particularly difficult to do so. I ask this honorable court to provide me with protection.

M. N.

from an affidavit, *A.K.T. and Others against the Minister of Law & Order and Others*

Shoot, You Have Already Shot My Son

His mother described what happened:

The green overalls [municipal police] arrived in their trucks and said they must remove the stones. The stones had been placed there for the football game—they were the goals—through which they would kick the ball. T. said: Let us finish this one game. There were four green overalls and one white man. I know them. Their names are: M. Y., M. J., Z. B., T. and Mr. N.—a white man.

Then all four green overalls grabbed K. H. [She] had been standing in her yard and had come out to see what was going on. They dragged her towards their van. I went to stand next to K. and tried to loosen their grip on her. T. was standing on the corner—the corner of the house. He said: The woman has done nothing—you can't put her in the van—she has done nothing.

T.'s father arrived and told him to come home—told him not to speak. T. began walking. Then M. started running. He grabbed a revolver from another green overall man's side. He ran towards T. and said: I'm going to shoot you. When T. heard this, he turned around. There was a loud noise. M. shot T. in the head. T. fell down.

Mr. N. said: Pick up that man you've injured. Then M. said to me: I'm going to shoot you now, old woman. He placed the revolver at my forehead. I said: Shoot, you've already shot. Then M. saw T.'s father—he said: Old man, have you something to say? I'm going to shoot you now. He placed the revolver at my husband's forehead. My husband said: Shoot, you have already shot my son.

M. turned around and climbed into the van. By this time T.'s body was already in the van. The green overalls had loaded him in.

N. M.

from Black Sash Archives

I Was Terrified

On July 27, 1985, I was asleep in the front room of my house when the police arrived at about 1 A.M. I was awoken by the sound of loud banging on the door, and before I could get out of bed the door was broken down and many policemen came into the house. There were both black and white policemen. They started shouting, and I think I heard the words "consumer boycott," but before anybody in the house was given the opportunity to say anything the police began to assault people.

I was terrified and simply sat on my bed in fear. As I was sitting on my bed a black policeman, Mr. N. S., began to hit me with the open palm of his hand. He slapped me twice in the face and then hit me with the back of his long gun. I still have the scar on the right-hand side of my nose from this blow.

My mother and father and other family members, all of whom were at home at the time, were assaulted by police who hit them with batons and sjamboks. I too was struck with both batons and sjamboks by Zulu policemen. I have a scar on my right cheek from a sjambok blow which was delivered by a Zulu policeman.

I was bleeding from the two cuts on my face and had pain from the bruises on my back from baton blows. I was also bleeding from my left ear.

I was the only person who was arrested from the house, and the police took me and loaded me in a private car and drove me to the police station. At the police station I was interrogated about who the instigator of the Fort Beaufort consumer boycott was. My fingerprints were taken, and I was later placed in the Land Rover and taken to the Fort Beaufort Prison. I was detained under the Emergency regulations for fourteen days and thereafter released. I was never charged. The assaults upon me and my family were cruel and needless. No one made any attempt to resist the police, and their behavior was completely unreasonable.

Z.M.

from Black Sash Archives

The Children Are Not Scared of Death

When you talk to the general people, sometimes they feel that they are scared to face politics in the open. Sometimes they want discussions privately. But not the children. They might already be spoiled because of the lack of education. But what little they have they'll use to fight—fight back for the whole history—for the days after the war when the British couldn't pay the Afrikaners who fought in the war, and so they paid with Africa—the children are not scared of death. They are just bold. They call us older people cowards.

Elizabeth Nelani

from *South African Women Speak*

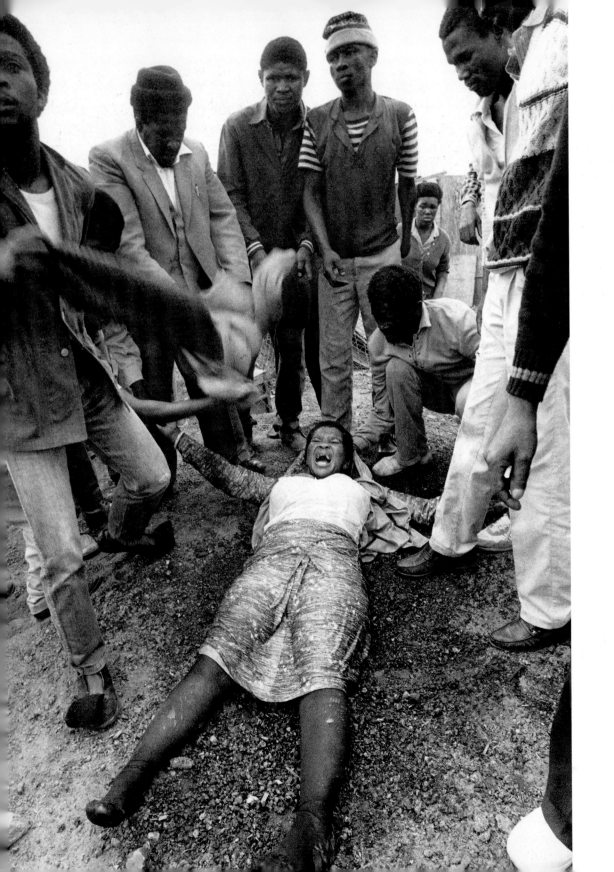

Left, a woman overcome by tear gas is helped by fellow mourners during the funeral for eight people killed in the "bottle-store (liquor-store) incident" in New Brighton township, Port Elizabeth, April 1986. Nearly a week before, on March 25, heavily-armed police hid in a liquor store that had been bombed the previous day. A crowd gathered, and the police opened fire, killing eight. Because they symbolize state power and have been the source of much anti-social behavior, liquor stores and beer halls are frequent targets for black anger. The eastern Cape, traditionally one of the most militant areas, has a long history of resistance. It was the birthplace of the African National Congress and the political home of Steve Biko and other Black Consciousness leaders in the 1970s.

Opposite, a Duduza township resident lies dead while members of a special police squad take a smoke break after an all night "cleanup," Transvaal, July 1985. Photographs such as this led to the government emergency regulations making it an offense to photograph police in "an unrest area or situation." The police have shot hundreds, and township residents cannot easily distinguish between national servicemen and covert death squads. The death squads usually wear woolen, hooded face covers, or masks, called "balaclavas," making it impossible to identify the killers. In this photograph, the man with his back turned still has his balaclava down.

This Poem Is Dedicated to Brother Andries Raditsela*

Your death has come to me over hundreds of miles away
It has shocked me but did not surprise me
It has shocked the workers but did not surprise them.

I have a few words to say—my mouth is a grave without flowers
My mouth is the empty coffin when the corpse is gone
It is like a river without water
But it has faith in your death.

If I had strength enough I would go and avenge your blood
Our blood
I would carry a bazooka and go straight for the murderers
I would go to the murderers' Concrete Capitals and shoot. . . .

Your blood, Andries, will not be in vain
Your blood will be a moral lesson for us to punish oppressors,

Treason, detention and murders
Your blood will give power to your comrades,
To the workers, to your family and to us all. . . .

Nise Malange

*Andries Raditsela—A shop steward in the Chemical Workers Industrial Union (CWIU)
who died in detention in 1985.

A man drags another tear gas victim to safety while clouds of tear gas rise in the background during the funeral for the people killed in the "bottle store incident" in New Brighton township, Port Elizabeth, April 1986.

Above, a mother says goodbye to her son as he prepares to flee their home to escape right-wing vigilantes in Leandra township, Transvaal, April 1986. Many Leandra children fled to Johannesburg, seeking refuge in churches and the homes of relatives in urban townships. Disrupted education and economic hardship are hazards in young lives.

Opposite, a schoolboy is arrested during the protests against the 1987 white parliamentary elections in Athlone township, Cape Town, May 1987. In 1986, some 25,000 people were imprisoned without trial under the Emergency regulations, and of that number, 10,000 were children under the age of eighteen. In April 1987, the government stated that only 1,400 children were still in detention. From September 23 to 27, 1987, a Conference on the Repression of Children in South Africa, held at the University of Zimbabwe in Harare, focused international attention on the issue of imprisoned children.

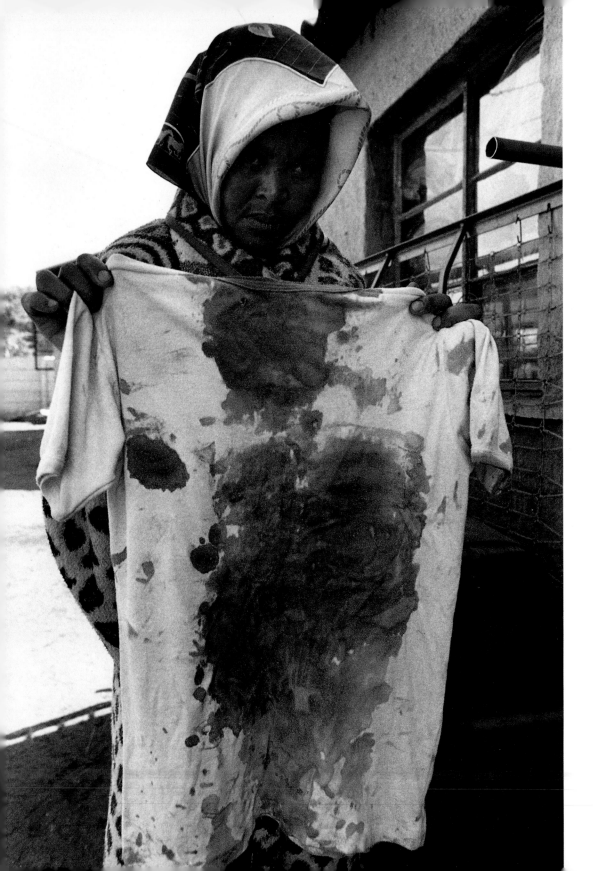

A mother holds up the bloodstained shirt of her son, shot in the back by police, Tembisa township, Transvaal, June 1985. According to government statistics, 381 people were killed in "unrest" incidents between September 1984 and April 1985. The government's own statistics acknowledge that three quarters of these victims died as a direct result of police action.

A Thabong youth shows the whip marks left on him by vigilantes in Welkom township, Orange Free State, June 1985. Vigilantes form menacing gangs to terrorize anti-apartheid activists. Often they enjoy police support. Vigilantes in different parts of the country are generally motivated by local political issues or conflicts in their areas. Although the reasons for violence may differ, these acts of brutality have common, often horrific results, and help the government in its attempt to suppress the democratic movement in South Africa.

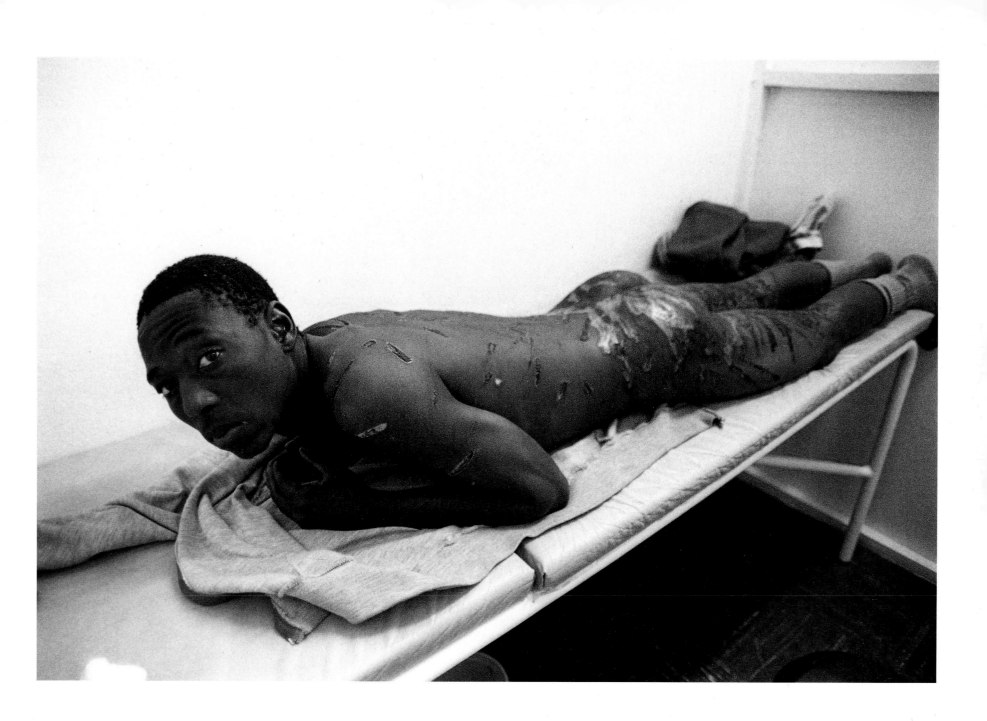

Opposite, members of the Leandra Youth Congress regroup after repelling an attack by vigilantes at the funeral of their community leader, Chief Ampie Mayisa, in Leandra township, Transvaal, 25 January 1986. Among the hundreds of grass-roots organizations, youth groups are quick to action in dangerous situations and vulnerable to vigilante attacks. Vigilantes represent a complex social phenomenon, but there is evidence that they receive direct state support, encouragement, and even protection.

Right, Gladys Sangweni is shown here sitting in the ruins of her home in Pietermaritzburg, 1988. Her husband was killed by vigilantes who had come to the house, looking for their son, a United Democratic Front activist. Three days earlier, her daughter had been killed in another township clash in Pietermaritzburg. The Sangweni family was faced with virtual annihilation in the bloody conflicts between Inkatha and the UDF. Many Pietermaritzburg families suffered overwhelming losses as the tension and battles continued, and by May 1989, over 1000 people had been killed.

A member of the Leandra Youth Congress, with arms extended and a stone in his hand, tries to ward off a heavily armed band of vigilantes. Leandra township has been the scene of terrible violence. In Leandra, many workers are migrants from rural areas, but others have been raised in the harsh urban environment of the township. When younger urban residents come into conflict with older, traditional peoples, the government has been able to exploit their differences for its own aims. Vigilantes threatened Mayisa and other leaders of the United Democratic Front-affiliated Leandra Action Committee one week before Mayisa's murder, but the police ignored calls for protection. The police respond to accusations of their complicity in vigilante violence by saying such charges are "nothing but attempts to discredit the police." Chief Mayisa's murderers have not yet been found.

Armed KwaZulu police keep a protective eye over an Inkatha (Zulu nationalist organization) rally on June 16, 1986, in Curries Fountain Soccer Stadium, Durban. Ironically, Inkatha has been permitted to hold rallies to commemorate the Soweto uprising of June 16, 1976, while organizations more closely identified with the legacy of the resistance symbolized by this date have been prevented from observing its anniversary.

Police reload after firing at mourners after the funeral for the young activists killed in the ''grenade incident'' in Duduza township, Transvaal, July 1985. In most cases when people face hostile armed troops, they have only stones for their defense. Bending down to pick up a stone can bring instant retaliation, and the victims of stray bullets have been numerous. Deaths follow funerals with sad predictability.

Why Did God Create a Human Being?

The situation in our townships is so disgusting that you sometimes ask yourself a question that has got no answer and that is, "Why did God create a human being?" We are always running away from the SADF troops. We are guarded every day by troops as if we are criminals who are life sentenced. We can no longer walk as free men on our own land. We are forced to carry heavy papers that cause suffering, hunger and sorrow to our people. When you move in each and every township you are forced to tiptoe, afraid of being seen by the "casspirs." Especially we boys. We have sleepless nights being afraid of being taken away from our families to slavery. Whenever you hear a knock on the door at night you start panicking without knowing why. All that comes into your mind at once is a man wearing a greenish helmet, green camouflage clothes, a pair of dark brown boots, a pistol in a holster on his waist and a rifle in his hands with a red face hunting you like a beast.

B., a 15-year-old boy
from *Two Dogs and Freedom: Children of the Townships Speak Out*

They Handcuffed Me and Chained Me

On 29th July 1985, I and a group of fellow students went to the Moroka police station to inquire when three of our colleagues would be released. I went in alone. When I tried to leave the police station I was stopped by two white plainclothes policemen. They handcuffed and chained me. After I had said that I had connections with COSAS [Congress of South African Students], the other policeman said that meant that I was a stone thrower. B. then demanded information about the whereabouts of other people whom he said were members of COSAS. When I said I did not know, some of the policemen kicked me and punched me while saying that I was lying.

A bucket filled with water was produced into which one of the policemen pumped tear gas. Another then forced my head into the bucket. My eyes began to water and I sneezed and coughed. My face felt as if it were burning. I was then ordered to remove my clothes and to stand on a wooden block. My face was covered with a United Democratic Front T-shirt. I felt metal clips being attached to each of my wrists. There followed a series of electric shocks which ran up my arms and caused great pain. This treatment lasted for about 5 minutes. My wrists still bear the scars of the burns caused by the shock treatment.

Still naked, I was made to lie on the floor with my face down. About ten bricks were then placed on my neck and back. Two of the policemen stood on the bricks and then jumped up and down on me. This lasted for about 20 minutes and caused great pain. The questions previously asked were repeated often. When I replied that I had no information to give, I was slapped, punched and kicked.

After about 2 weeks I was taken to the New Johannesburg Prison at Diepkloof. Upon my arrival, I was assaulted by several prison warders wielding rubber batons. I was placed in solitary confinement for about 14 days. When I was released from solitary confinement, I was placed in a large cell where I met SRM and KF. Both asked me whether I had been tortured and assaulted there [Protea Police Station]. Both said that they had been. S.R.M. and K.F. were taken to the Protea Police Station for further interrogation.

On one occasion, when S.R.M. returned, one of his eyes was swollen and black. He also cradled a limp arm which he said had been broken when one of the policemen at the Protea Police Station had ordered him to stand on a table and had then pulled his legs from under him, causing him to fall forward onto the ground and crush his arms. When K.F. returned from one of his visits to the Protea Police Station, his neck was severely swollen and his vision was impaired. He said that he had been beaten repeatedly on the head and in his face and eyes.

S.M., a 17-year-old boy,
from a signed affidavit

The Tear Gas Was Too Much

On 15th September 1985 I attended the funeral of L.N. I have the same mother as L.N., and I spoke at the church and at the grave. When I was in the police van the police sprayed tear gas about three times through the mesh with aerosols. The van did not have windows. The tear gas was too much because they sprayed it on my clothes and in my face. I was coughing, and then I think I lost consciousness. Then I was taken to Swift grounds, where the police have tents. This is where I was tortured. They took me to a tent. Then there was an iron bar there—they handcuffed me to the iron with my hands behind my back. Then they started to hit and kick me. There were four white men who were not in uniform. There was also another man who I think is a police captain. After the other policemen had already hit my face, the "captain" said they must not hit my face, they should keep the hits on my body. They kept on hitting me and then threw water at me.

Then the police left me standing there handcuffed to the iron bar. I think they went to eat. Then the same four men came back and started to hit me again. I lost consciousness, and when I woke up I found I was in a police van. They took me back to Swift grounds. There they left me to sleep in the van. They threw water into the van, and I had to sleep in the water. I stayed like this the whole night. I had no shirt and no blankets. They took me again to Church Street Police Station. They handcuffed me again and put a rope around my neck. They pulled the rope tight and demanded that I tell them where I bought the T-shirt. I replied that somebody had given it to me at the funeral. My eye is still red from the beating, and my ear is very painful. My ribs are painful, and I am not feeling all right.

Z.T., an 18-year-old boy,
from a signed affidavit

Some of Us Fainted

Then on 29 November 1985, I was still sleeping at home when 6 or 7 policemen came to our house. They told me to get dressed and come with them and they will bring me back. Then they picked up some other children—we were many—and took us to the police station. At the police station, we were taken to the yard. On the third floor there were people hiding and pointing out the children. When they finished this, we were put into the cells. So late that afternoon, they took our fingerprints, and 40 of us were taken to the Ladismith Police Station. We were held there for the weekend. On that Monday, we had to see the magistrate. That is when the magistrate took our case at the police station and said we must wait until 18 December 1985. That day we were not given our charges. They said they would give the charges on Wednesday. On Wednesday I was told my charge is for murder.

During the second week in the cells, I was sick. I had a bad stomach. I asked a policeman to take me to a doctor. He said he would take me to a doctor that day, but he only took me the next day. I had two injections and was given some pills and then taken back to the cells.

Early one morning, some policemen told us to get up because they were going to clean the cells. When they returned to our cell, we were making our beds and tidying up, but they said we were slow and they sprayed tear gas into the cell. And then later they sprayed water which made the blankets and mats wet. Then they sprayed the tear gas. They locked us in a closed cell. Some of us fainted, and some of us vomited. I vomited. The others with me in the cell were all young; one was nine years old, others 10 and 11 years. That night the mats were wet, so were the blankets. We slept on the wet mats.

There was a second occasion when they put tear gas to us. There was singing in another cell. Then they came to our cell and sprayed tear gas into the cell.

Then the third time there was some clash between a policeman and people in another cell, and they were told to put tear gas in our cell too. So they sprayed tear gas in our cell.

Sometimes the policemen came at night and kicked us and woke us up. There were black and white policemen. I was also kicked by Mr. N. who is a policeman I know.

I was held in the cells for 21 days. During this time I did not see my mother. She brought food and clothing for me, but I was not allowed to see her.

The food they gave us was old bread and a little moerkoffie in the morning. In the afternoon they gave us soup which tasted bad, and then for supper they gave us that little coffee and old bread. More than once, we threw this food into the bucket. The policemen then said if we don't take this food, then we will not get our food from our parents. So we took the food.

On 18 December 1985, I was released on free bail and told to appear in court on 21 January 1986.

J. M., a 14-year-old boy
from *The Last Affidavits*

I Heard Loud Knocking

On Friday, 9 October 1987, I was asleep at home in the little hut which serves as the kitchen where I stayed with my mother, younger brothers and sisters. My mother, A.M., was in the main hut asleep with my sisters. Late that night I heard people knocking at the door of my mother's hut, demanding that she open the door. I heard them shouting the word "maqabane" (comrade) [youth or young person]. I felt very scared when I heard the visitors go into her hut and the sound of men shouting. Moments later I heard loud knocking at the door of my hut. I asked who was knocking. My mother responded that I should open the door. When I opened the door many men entered the hut with my mother. I was able to identify them. [Names seven men.] My sister P. followed this group.

I know the first man because he is our Induna [chief]. I also know him because he has come to our school on a number of occasions to address us on Inkatha. In this regard I can remember him dividing the school into Inkatha members and non-Inkatha members. When all of the Inkatha members were on the one side he would tell the rest of us that unless we joined Inkatha he would come with other Inkatha boys and deal with us. This was a threat that I and my friends have always taken seriously.

Most of the men were carrying guns. I noticed that when the first man came into the room he was carrying a small gun in his hand and the other man had a long gun which had a shoulder strap. Eventually the men returned to my mother's hut and said that they were satisfied that my brothers were not there, and they announced they were leaving. I heard my mother say that she was going to relieve herself. I then heard the first man say to my mother that she should not move and should lean against the wall. I heard a gunshot and heard her groan. I think there was another shot; however, I am not sure. After they shot my mother I heard someone tell her to get up and open the door. I did not hear her answer as I hid under my bed.

A short while later one of the men entered the room. I saw a man aim his gun at my sister P. and fire one shot. She fell to the floor, and I heard more shots. I remember her crying out "Asu weMa." ("Oh, my mother.") She lay bleeding on the floor. She was moaning. I closed my eyes, and after a short while the men went outside, and I heard the first man say that they should burn the house. One of the men argued against this, saying that they already had two of us. A few minutes later my other sister came into the room. We fled from the hut and ran into the bush far from the house, where we spent that night. It was cold, and as we were only wearing very light clothes we piled dry grass on top of us and hugged each other to keep warm.

K.M., a 13-year-old boy,
from a signed affidavit

Thomas Mandla Shabalala, Inkatha Central
Committee member, leads an anti-COSATU
(Congress of South African Trade Unions)
parade at the launch of Inkatha's trade union
wing, the United Workers Union of South
Africa (UWUSA), Durban, May Day 1986.
It was in the Natal region that the democratic
trade union movement first built its strength
after the mass strikes of 1973. Inkatha has
also staked its claim to the allegiance of Zulus in the area, based on an appeal to ethnic
tradition. While many Zulu workers have divided COSATU/Inkatha loyalties, Inkatha's
efforts to launch a rival union have met with
negligible results despite the government's
support. For the event in this picture, rural
chiefs were instructed to fill buses with their
people, and special trains brought Inkatha
supporters to the UWUSA rally. To complete the extravaganza, Chief Buthelezi arrived in a helicopter. Nonetheless, UWUSA
did not "bury" COSATU, just as all the
government's efforts to dismantle the democratic, non-racial workers' federation have
failed.

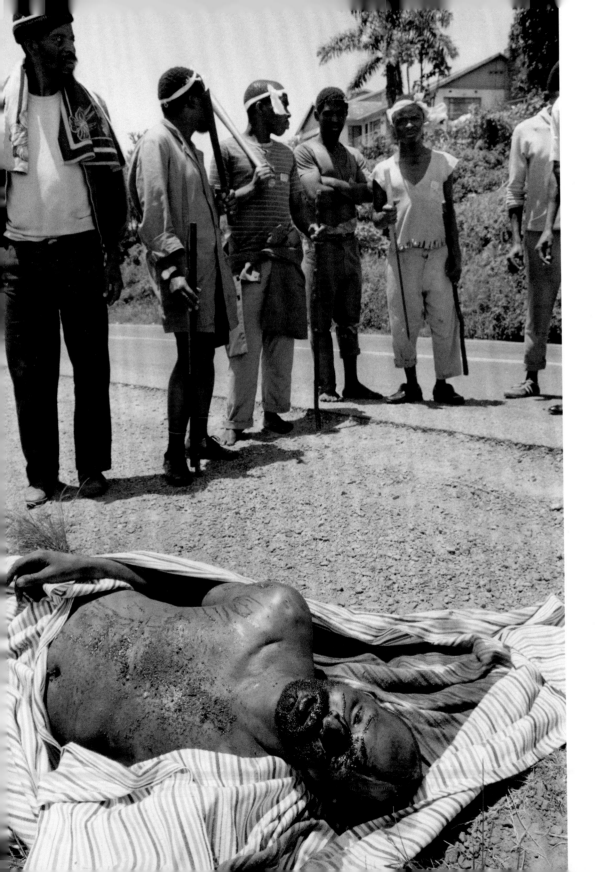

Left, members of a Zulu *impi* stand over the body of a Pondo man, killed during clashes between the two groups, Umbogintwini, Natal, January 1986. Neither the Pondos nor the Zulus can survive in their respective rural homelands where the government has sent them, and they have established massive squatter settlements on the outskirts of Durban to be closer to jobs. Under harsh living conditions in the over-populated squatter settlements, conflicts between different peoples are inevitable. Zulus and Pondos fight over the few jobs and scarce resources allowed them by the government.

Opposite, vigilantes, unopposed by the police, set fire to homes in Crossroads, a squatter township near Cape Town, May 1986. Crossroads is the original and most famous of the many squatter townships that grew up in areas where blacks migrated, searching for work. Under apartheid, the government prohibited the building of houses for blacks in restricted urban areas, but people continued to flock to them in hope of employment. As squatter towns grew, the government would bulldoze them and send the inhabitants back to impoverished homelands. Because of its homeland policy, the government considers blacks temporary residents in the white cities, but in defiance of the influx control laws, migrant workers bring their families from impoverished rural areas to live with them. In the 1980s the state changed its strategy of direct forced removals with its associated bad publicity to more covert methods. The government encouraged vigilantes. In Crossroads where the government had used bulldozers to dislocate residents, it began to support resident-collaborators, *Witdoeke* (white-headband) vigilantes, to further its aims. An estimated 80,000 people were left homeless and 60 dead as a result of Witdoeke action in 1986.

We learnt from the pain and sorrow of
having lost our children to so many and such cruel
deaths as malnutrition or murder or sadness even
dying while throwing spears or stones and being
shot dead. we can now say, while we claim our
land and die in the process: our history is a culture
of resistance

Mongane Serote
from *Time Has Run Out*

A Pondo woman sits in the ruins of her
home, burned out during clashes between
Zulus and Pondos, Umbogintwini, Natal,
January 1986. In this region of Natal, the
Zulus are the dominant ethnic group, and the
Pondo people have migrated here from the
Transkei in their search for work. Transkei,
the largest and oldest of the so-called homelands, is hopelessly overcrowded, and unemployment there is so high that thousands of
Pondo people have migrated, building large
shantytowns near urban areas. The Zulus,
threatened by this heavy influx of Pondos
into their territories, resort to violence
against the newcomers, turning some shantytowns almost into war zones. The apartheid
system is the catalyst for what the government expediently labels ''intertribal''
conflict.

Women from Crossroads squatter camp demonstrate outside Parliament, demanding protection from witdoeke (white-headband) vigilantes and for the right to rebuild their burnt-out homes, Cape Town, June 1986. At the beginning of the 1980s, a women's organization, *Nomzamo* (She Who Struggles), led the broad democratic movement that attempted to win control of Crossroads. The defeat of the women's movement in the region paved the way for the victory of the vigilante boss, Ngxobongwana.

A lone woman protests as the soldiers occupying her township roll by in large armored military vehicles called ''hippos,'' Soweto, July 1985. Women have played a significant role against the army's occupation of the townships. In Chesterville, a township near Durban, women nightly patrolled the streets to protect families from security force and vigilante harassment. Popular women leaders like Albertina Sisulu, Dorothy Nyembe, and Frances Baard have inspired many.

Under repressive state restrictions funerals have become the settings for mass political rallies. Emotions run high on these sad occasions as people grieve for the dead and renew their commitment to resist the government. Huge African National Congress banners are unfurled, and coffins draped with ANC colors remind the participants of the political causes of the deaths. The funerals are also marked by moving oratory. While Archbishop Tutu may appeal for restraint, others will speak with uncompromisingly militant words, like the poet who recited:

God forgives. I don't.
Africa, do something.
The spear has fallen.
Pick it up!

The crowds participating in the funerals sing political songs and perform militant new dances, turning the funerals themselves into remarkable forms of political and cultural expression.

Often the mourners are honoring civilians, including children, who have died in street confrontations with the armed forces. Or, the dead are victims of stray bullets. Increasingly, they have included members of the UDF, community leaders, or members of Umkhonto we Sizwe, the ANC's military wing. The deaths of Umkhonto members indicate a new, armed dimension to the resistance movement.

Since 1986, official restrictions have been imposed on the funerals of "unrest" victims in many parts of the country under the State of Emergency. "Authorized" mourners are issued stamped police permits and are limited to 200 in number. Similarly, the funerals themselves are restricted to three hours, and police must approve the time, date, and place. Public address systems are banned; only ordained ministers may speak; and flags, posters, and pamphlets are forbidden. Police usually maintain a high profile at funerals in an attempt to intimidate the crowd. Police action, forcibly dispersing mourners, is common, and many services come to an abrupt, chaotic conclusion when police throw tear gas at the gathering. Police justify their disruptions because the mourners typically infringe the official funeral regulations.

The funerals are testimonies to the many politically related deaths in South Africa. Since September 1984, over 4,000 South Africans, primarily black victims, have died in violent incidents. Researchers at the University of Natal in Durban have reported that "factional struggles accounted for 1,848 deaths and that 1,113 other township residents were killed by South African forces deployed to suppress political unrest" (The New York Times, Sunday, March 5, 1989, p. 4).

Editors' note

A mother mourns the death of her two sons, killed in a clash with an Inkatha impi in Mphophomeni, near Pietermaritzburg, Natal, 1987. Mphophomeni is a resettlement area for people who were forcibly removed from other regions. The core of the community consists of families of workers for BTR-Sarmcol, an international company whose labor practices in the region led to a prolonged strike. Many workers joined the Metal and Allied Workers Union, a strong and politically active union. Some activists have been the victims of Inkatha violence.

Carrying symbolic rifles, mourners stand over the coffins of Queenstown residents killed in an incident known as the "Queenstown massacre," when police opened fire outside a church where people were meeting to discuss a consumer boycott, Queenstown, eastern Cape, December 1985. A United Democratic Front pamphlet, announcing the funeral, said, "On Sunday, 17 November 1985, 14 people were brutally murdered as they were coming from a legal community meeting held at Nonzwakazi church. Our strongest words of condemnation could not match the senseless killings of our comrades." The dead included three fifteen-year-olds.

In the image, a sign reads:

PAX BIN
IN LOVING MEMORY
OF OUR DEAREST
MTHUZELELI ROGER
REMEMBERED BY FAMILY
DIED: 17·02·86
AGED 25
REST IN PEACE SON OF AFRICA

A youth brandishing a wooden rifle heads the funeral procession of an African National Congress soldier, Roger Fortuin, killed in a shootout with police, Joza township, Grahamstown, February 1986. Following decades of protest politics and Gandhian passive resistance, directly influenced by the Mahatma's sojourn in South Africa at the beginning of the century, the ANC felt compelled to take up arms in the early 1960s after the Sharpeville massacre and its banning along with other political organizations. The ANC formed a military wing, Umkhonto we Sizwe, which means "Spear of the Nation." Umkhonto directs nearly all of its actions against state and military targets.

Within a month the ''sensitive situation'' had become a bloody one—Chief Mayisa was to be hacked to death by vigilantes who also called for the blood of Nkabinde and burnt his house. At the chief's funeral and afterwards, further violence was to erupt.

from *Mabangalala*

The son of Chief Ampie Mayisa, leading the singing and chanting mourners, defends his father's funeral cortege from vigilante attack, Leandra township, Transvaal, January 1986. Mayisa led his community successfully in its fight against forced removal. Although he sought police protection against vigilantes, he was murdered by them soon after the police denied his appeal. Right-wing vigilante groups emerged in many communities that were resisting removal.

Vigilantes

The term "vigilante" (or "Mabangalala") has come to have a distinct meaning in South Africa. It does not mean a concerned citizen intent on preserving the safety of his family and "decent values." In South Africa, the term "vigilante" has a far more menacing connotation. It is associated with potentially murderous gangs, intent on intimidating, injuring or killing anti-apartheid activists. That, and the fact that they are believed to enjoy police support, is very often all that binds the "A-team," the "Pakhatis," the "Mabangalala," the "Amadoda," the "Amosolomzi," the "Amabutho," the "Mbhokoto" and the "Green Berets."

The motivation and composition of these vigilante groups vary according to the specific politics of the area. But the common fear that activist and human rights campaigners share is best illustrated by a few random examples of vigilante action.

Mr. B.M., a supporter of the United Democratic Front, who lives in Umlazi was at home one evening in August 1985 when a large group of armed men ("Amabutho") surrounded his house and set it alight.

I woke immediately the fire started but was unable to escape from the house without being burnt in my back, arms and face. My younger brother, M., jumped through the window of my mother's bedroom and turned to take my sister's infant child from my sister. As he took the child, he was shot by a member of the armed mob which surrounded him. He was shot in the head. He fell to the ground and dropped the baby. My mother grabbed both of them and pulled them into the bushes around the house. I also hid in the bushes and watched as our house burnt. I noticed three men standing around the house holding guns. My elder sister, F., was also shot by a member of the mob as she tried to escape from the flames.

They Wanted to Kill Me

I saw a group of people coming to my house and saw that they were armed with pangas [long knives], kieries [sticks] and shovels. I recognized them as members of Inkatha [Zulu nationalist organization]. They approached the house, and they said they wanted to kill me. Fortunately, there was a group of supporters of the LAC [UDF-affiliated Leandra Action Committee] at my house at the time. Some of the intruders approached me with pangas, and the members of my group clashed with them, whereupon they left. However, J. Z. turned back and came towards me pulling a firearm out of his trouser band. He pointed it at me. When he saw that there were too many witnesses and LAC supporters on the scene, he eventually departed.

A.N.

I Asked for Mercy

My eyes were covered by someone placing his hands over them, and they asked me how they should kill me. I was given three choices, namely, that they either burn me, stab me or shoot me. When J. Z. held a gun to my forehead, they uncovered my eyes and said that I should choose in which manner I wished them to kill me. He repeated the choices. I asked for mercy, and J. Z. told me that I would not be left alone and that I must make my choice as I was a follower of the late Chief Mayisa.

J.N.

I Fear for My Life

I was accused of allowing the United Democratic Front-affiliated KwaMashu Youth League to meet in my church. I was made to walk down the road in broad daylight. Many of the men were armed. I was forced to wave my fist in the air, and chant, "The UDF is a dog." About a hundred yards from my home, I saw Mr. T. of the Lindelani area. He is a well-known Inkatha figure. He was with a large crowd of armed men. Only when I agreed to come to the stadium on the following Sunday, did they agree to release me. I no longer live in KwaMashu as I fear for my life.

W. M.

The House Was Burning

One Monday evening, in August 1985, the KwaMashu Youth League met as usual in G Section in the Methodist church. During the course of the meeting, about 90 Inkatha supporters came to the church and began chanting and singing the praise of their chief. As members of the KwaMashu Youth League left the church, they were chased and dispersed by the Inkatha group. On 10 September 1985, a group of armed men petrol-bombed the house of Mrs. M. I telephoned the Durban Central Fire Brigade, and I was referred to the Umhlanga Fire Station. I telephoned this station, who referred me back to the Durban station. I telephoned the Durban station and spoke to a Mr. O. He said that he first had to get clearance from his superiors as to whether he could take up a complaint in KwaMashu because I fell under the jurisdiction of the KwaZulu Development Corporation. He said thereafter he had to telephone the KwaMashu police to ask them to go to the scene to confirm that there was indeed a fire. He said only then could he send his men. I said the house was burning at that very moment and that by the time he had gone through the necessary procedures, the house would be burned down to the ground, which it did.

S.K.

from *Mabangalala: The Rise of Right Wing Vigilantes in South Africa*

The Police Are There

At about 11 A.M. a big crowd of people—men, women and children—fled from the Portlands Cement squatter camp to our squatter camp. We asked the people what is going on, and they said to us, "The police are there, they are shooting, and the people from Old Crossroads are also there shooting." At about 12 o'clock we saw two casspirs [armoured military vehicles] driving in front of a crowd of about 200 men armed with guns, axes, pangas [long knives] and kieries [sticks] advancing towards us. The men were wearing white doeks [bands] on their heads and around their arms. I recognized them as Old Crossroads residents who formed part of the Ngxobongwana/Ndima camp. The policemen in the casspirs did absolutely nothing to stop them in their plundering and burning of houses. We took fright and ran away to a distance of about 50 meters from where we saw them setting our houses on fire. We ran back to try and protect our property but were shot at both by members of the witdoeke [white head-band vigilantes] and the police, of whom there might have been about a hundred. We had no guns and only sticks to protect ourselves with.

M.M.Y.

I Observed the Fighting

During the whole of Sunday, then, I observed the fighting between the "witdoeke" and the other groupings who were living on the land from which we were driven that day. I was shocked not only by the violence and the unprovoked attack of the vigilantes, or the witdoeke, but by the role of the South African police during that day. From my observation, the South African police actively sided with and supported the "witdoeke" against us, and it was also apparent to me that the South African police had no interest whatsoever in stopping the fighting. This they could have done quite easily by arresting, disarming, driving off the "witdoeke" forces, but they made no attempt to do so whatsoever. Instead, they directed their forces against the groups which the "witdoeke" were attacking.

Early in the morning I saw casspirs filled with SADF [South African Defense Force] men and SADF members on foot firing firebombs into our camp. They would fire projectiles from something which was like a gun. When it landed, it would explode, and there would be flames, and very often these flames would cause shacks to catch fire. I know that these people firing these bombs were members of the South African Defense Force because of the uniforms which they were wearing which were of khaki color. These soldiers were accompanied by "witdoeke," and there were absolutely no hostilities between these soldiers and the "witdoeke." They were working hand in hand together.

S.M.

from affidavits from Cape Town Legal Resources Centre
on the Crossroads/KTC conflict

An African National Congress flag bearer heads the procession at the funeral of a United Democratic Front activist shot by police in Guguletu, a black township outside of Cape Town, December 1986. This procession is almost emblematic of South African resistance, led by the ANC, the Church, and the UDF, with the message, ''The People Shall Govern.''

The souls of those killed cry out, "How long Lord is this going to continue?" The answer is the time is not right until some more of you, brothers and sisters, are killed. The price we have paid already is a heavy price. We are being called on to pay yet more in lives. But despite all that the powers of the world may do, we are going to be free.

**Archbishop Tutu
from a funeral speech**

Archbishop Desmond Tutu speaks out against "necklace" killings at a funeral in KwaThema township, Transvaal, July 1986. The first necklace killing occurred on 23 March 1985, two days after the Langa massacre in the eastern Cape. It was of a town councilor in KwaNobuhle who had been accused of leading vigilante attacks and working with the South African police. Necklace killings as violent forms of revenge were out of control of democratic organizations like the United Democratic Front and church groups, which try to stop them. Only after the UDF, the ANC, and other popular groups condemned necklacing did it stop.

Opposite, mourners grieve at the funeral of members of the Thulani family, shot dead when gunmen burst into the home of Willis Ntuli, a lay preacher, and opened fire, Kwa-Makhuta township, Natal, February 1987. The gunmen were looking for Ntuli's son, Eric, a United Democratic Front activist, who had already fled. The Thulanis had stayed overnight at the Ntuli home after an all-night prayer service. KwaMakhuta is a huge squatter settlement outside of Durban where there are intense clashes between Zulu and Pondo people over scarce resources. In this case, the issue was political, reflecting the struggle between Inkatha and the UDF for influence and control in the Natal region.

Top right, accompanied by members of the Port Elizabeth Youth Congress, the father of Brian Mosita, one of eight people killed in the "bottle-store (liquor-store) incident," grieves for his son, New Brighton township, Port Elizabeth, April 1986.

Bottom right, young pallbearers stand at solemn attention at the funeral of three boys killed in the "Trojan Horse incident," when police, hiding in the back of a van, opened fire on a crowd, Cape Town, 1985.

On 16 July 1987, Peter Sello Motau, thirty-two years old, was gunned down in Swaziland by South African agents. Motau was a dedicated young activist who had joined the African National Congress in 1976, living in exile since his departure from Soweto on Christmas Eve 1975. Motau attended high school in Soweto where he was active in politics. His father had been detained early in the 1970s for alleged participation in ANC activities but was acquitted. After Peter left Soweto, his parents never heard from him again until they received a telegram from the ANC informing them of his death. Motau's mother went to Swaziland to arrange for the delivery of her son's body to Maputo where he had been living with his wife and two children, while his father tried to get a passport to travel to Maputo for the funeral. Ultimately, his family was able to arrange for the return of his body to Soweto. His mother is shown in this picture mourning his death at a severely restricted funeral in her home in Soweto. In leaving Soweto at the age of eighteen to join the ANC, Peter Motau is an example of the politicization of black school-children of his generation. Although he left in 1975, many others left Soweto after the 1976 uprising to join the ANC in exile.

Opposite, police watch as mourners carrying an African National Congress flag pass by during the funeral of eight youths killed during clashes between police and residents in Alexandra township. Off-duty township police allegedly killed three in reprisals following attacks on the policemen's homes, and five were killed by police during subsequent protests against vigilante action, Johannesburg, May 1986.

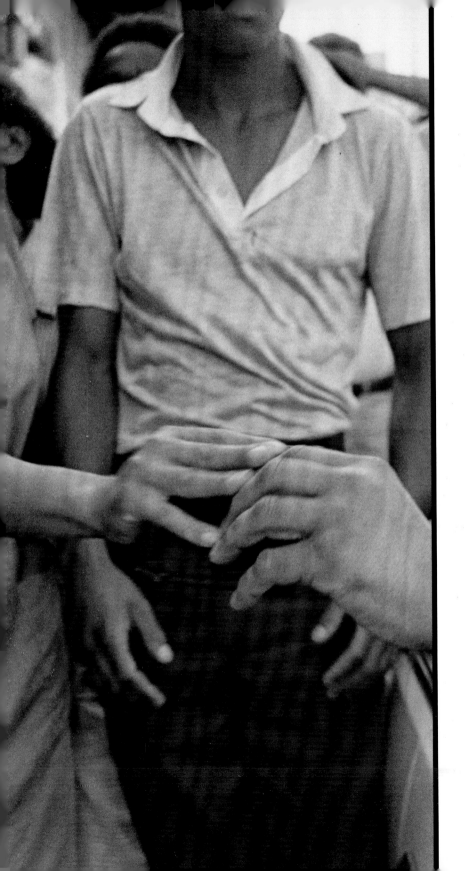

He Was Beaten to Death

Peter Nchabeleng died less than 48 hours after he was arrested at his home and taken to Schoonoord station by Lebowa policemen. The police have stated that the death resulted from a heart attack. Nchabeleng's family asserts that he was beaten to death, a claim which is supported by some evidence.

The victim was a well-known elder statesman of anti-apartheid politics and a regional leader of the United Democratic Front, currently the most prominent internal opposition group. In the 1960s he served an eight-year prison sentence alongside Nelson Mandela for "furthering the aims of the African National Congress," and had been intermittently banned thereafter. Nchabeleng reportedly had received numerous death threats for his activism over the years, and in 1983 was the target of a letter bomb, which was detected by friends and defused.

The arrest and subsequent death of the UDF *patron* took place amidst a concerted campaign against the organization by Lebowa officials, and in the wake of serious unrest in the region. Though a well-known advocate of nonviolence, Nchabeleng ostensibly was taken into custody on April 10 in connection with several "necklacings" in a nearby town. Mrs. Nchabeleng described to the Lawyers Committee what happened that morning:

It was still dark. I heard car doors slamming, and then people opening the building next door to look for our son Maurice, [who is] also an activist. When they couldn't find him they came over to where Peter and I were staying and banged on the door. There were about 5 or 10 of them, black policemen, some in uniforms and others in plain clothes. They had guns. After they had roused Peter out of bed, they told him to get dressed quickly and come with them. While they were waiting for him to dress they started saying, "Today we are going to kill you," and "We are going to kill you, you bloody whitehead" [a reference to Nchabeleng's age]. One of them said, "The child you killed, we are going to make you eat him" [an apparent reference to one of the "necklace" victims]. Peter denied participating in violence, saying he was a UDF member and not a criminal. Then they started asking him when he had joined the UDF, and also questions about the Lutheran Reverend M., and where the money Peter made from his coal business was going.

They also accused my husband of hiding guns, which he denied. The police searched the house but didn't find anything except books, letters, and the Freedom Charter, which they took. I remember Peter telling them that the Freedom Charter wasn't banned anymore. They then took him away. They never said why.

On Friday, April 11, Mrs. Nchabeleng received word from released detainees that her husband had been taken to Schoonoord Police Station. The next day, she heard from Reverend M. that Peter had died, a fact confirmed by two Lebowa policemen who visited her the same afternoon:

I asked the men who came if they'd killed Peter. They said no, that he had been ill in his heart and that they hadn't done anything to him. When they said this, I told them to their faces that he had never had heart problems and that he was in good health, because he was.

For the next week, the body of Mr. Nchabeleng became inaccessible to anyone but the police. His wife described her ordeal:

One of the policemen who told me of Peter's death said the body was at Phokwane mortuary, but when I got there, an official told me that the corpse had been taken to Groblersdal. He also told me that he'd seen the docket, and that Peter had died of natural causes.

We were getting ready to go to Groblersdal the next day when the Lebowa police arrived at my home and said the body was in Pretoria.

In Pretoria they didn't know about the body, but while we were there we read a story in the newspaper that said the corpse was in Pietersburg. In Pietersburg the people at the mortuary said they didn't know where my husband was.

After many days—it must have been over a week—our lawyer located the body in Groblersdal. I was then finally able to identify it.

The state pathologist's report is unavailable to the public, but Mr. Haysom [the family's lawyer] has had access to it. His decision to forgo a second independent inspection has been interpreted by the press as an indication that the document supports the family's allegations of murder. The only other source of information about the physical condition of the corpse is Mrs. Nchabeleng, who identified it. She states that she saw blood in the corpse's eyes, along with other visible marks, that confirmed her belief that he was beaten to death.

Other facts support Mrs. Nchabeleng's belief that her husband was a victim of police brutality. Several ex-detainees have told the family that they witnessed Peter being tortured at Schoonoord. Also, the Lebowa police have released a statement, purportedly written by Nchabeleng while in custody, urging conciliation toward all government security forces in the area. Assuming its authenticity, both the contents of this remarkable document and the wobbly signature beneath it suggest that the UDF leader was under tremendous duress while in the hands of his captors.

No date has yet been set for the inquest. Meanwhile, Nchabeleng's funeral has been held, on Lebowan soil. Attended by an estimated 30,000 mourners, the service was closely monitored by government aircraft and threatened with assault by a joint force of Lebowan and South African police until South African officers were physically presented with a court order authorizing the gathering. The deceased's 21-year-old son Maurice, arrested by the police on the same grounds as his father, was refused permission to attend.

from *Deaths in Custody: Seven Recent Cases*

Quite a Handful Disappeared without a Trace

The township was heavily patrolled especially by members of the riot unit. Shooting incidents increased by day. Many innocent victims were being shot by the police day and night, and many were arrested and detained. Those who had to receive treatment in a hospital were kept under police guard and prosecuted when discharged from hospital. Quite a handful disappeared without trace. A number of people were also killed in the shooting incidents. Funerals of victims followed. The authorities, especially the police, interfered with the course of events flowing from the killings. The families of the dead were served with orders issued under the security legislation compelling them to bury the dead during weekdays and not during weekends, as is customarily the case. Vigils held all around the township and well attended by residents were disrupted by the police. Tear gas was thrown at the houses in question in the dead of night, and when people ran out of a house they were shot and some beaten.

During the day a great number of people from the townships went to the courts to look for their next of kin and relatives who had disappeared. Some were found and some not. Those found were all charged with public violence.

A number of persons (about 8 in all) were shot by the police and killed in KwaNobuhle during the second week of March 1985. Of these victims, 3 were to be buried by their families. The police gave orders to the families concerned to bury each victim on three consecutive dates—21, 22 and 23 March 1985. The residents angrily demanded that they all be buried in one mass funeral on Saturday, 23 March 1985. The workers made it clear at the same time that if the funerals were to be held on the three dates mentioned above, they would stay away from work on Thursday and Friday, 21 and 22 March 1985, and attend the funerals. The workers were aware and angered by the fact that their white foremen were police reservists who did shooting at night in the townships and came back to the factory floor on the following morning to wave jubilantly the clock cards of some of those workers who were not at work and therefore presumed to be victims. As a result of the proposed stay away from the work place by workers, management became worried for obvious reasons. It is known that they tried to prevail on the authorities concerned not to ban weekend funerals.

The result was that on Wednesday, 20 March 1985, at night the police went to the three families concerned and advised them that they would be allowed to bury their dead jointly on Sunday, 24 March 1985, in KwaNobuhle. This announcement was not well received by the families who had by then finalized their funeral arrangements. Nonetheless, they felt powerless to defy the last-minute change for the reason that their dead were in fact in police custody at government mortuaries and could be released to them for burial when the police chose to do so.

from *A Short Background to Shooting Incident in Langa Township, Uitenhage*

We, the people of South Africa, declare for all our country and the world to know:—
That South Africa belongs to all who live in it, black and white, and that no government can justly claim authority unless it is based on the will of the people.

from the preamble to the *Freedom Charter*

Eastern Cape United Democratic Front leader Mathew Goniwe salutes the crowd at the funeral of youth activist Tamasanque Steven, Joza township, Grahamstown, 1986. Two months later, Mathew Goniwe, together with three other UDF leaders, was assassinated. Their mysterious deaths strengthened the perception that death squads had become an inseparable part of South African life. The car in which the four men were traveling was intercepted on a rural road. Before they drove off, they told friends that they would not stop unless ordered to do so by police. Police involvement is suspected in these brutal murders. The bodies were mutilated and burned, and the car moved to another location in an attempt to conceal evidence. The police insisted the deaths resulted from local political feuds and sternly reprimanded UDF leaders for jumping to other conclusions. The magistrate found at the inquest that their deaths were "caused by a person or persons unknown." Goniwe's assassination removed one of the most prominent and charismatic young leaders that the eastern Cape had produced since the death in detention of Steve Biko.

Above, police confront mourners at the funeral of eight people shot by security forces during the ''bottle-store (liquor-store) incident'' in New Brighton township, Port Elizabeth, April 1986. The funeral ended in chaos when police threw tear gas and violently dispersed the large crowd of mourners.

Opposite, pallbearers carrying coffins draped in African National Congress flags file through the crowd at the mass funeral of seven youths killed in a police ambush in Guguletu township, Cape Town, September 1986. Eyewitnesses alleged that several were shot at point-blank range when they were lying wounded on the road.

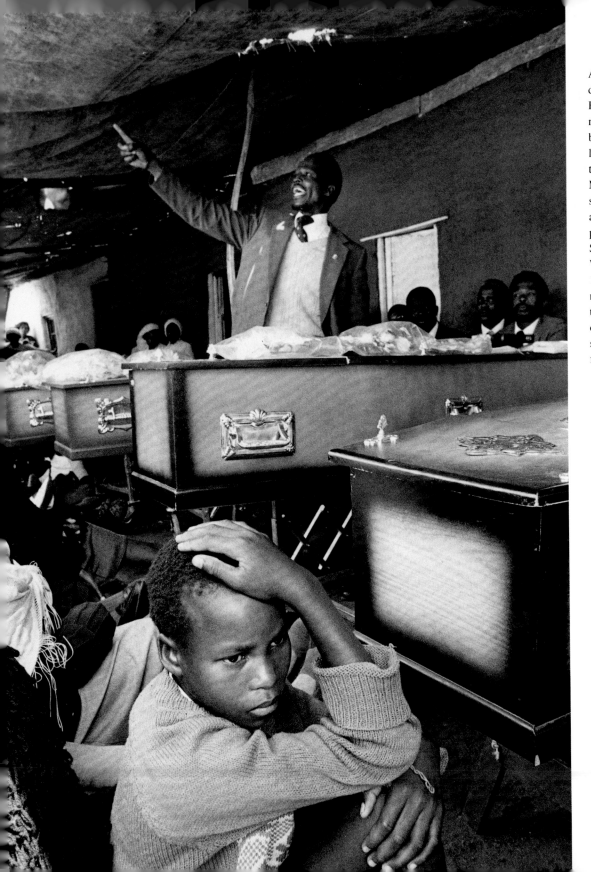

A speaker at the funeral of four people murdered by drunken municipal policemen in Fingo Village township, Grahamstown, February 1987. Besides tacitly and at times visibly encouraging counterrevolutionary vigilante groups, the government began in 1986 to recruit and arm more black policemen. Many of these police are *kitskonstabels* (instant constables) with little training. There are also black regular and armed municipal policemen and black soldiers in both the South African Defense Force and the South West African Territorial Force. At the end of 1987, strikes by municipal police and mutinies by black soldiers as well as the conviction of two black security policemen accused of spying for the African National Congress, suggested that the state's control of these forces is not absolute.

Mourners carry the coffin of one of eight youths killed in clashes with police in Alexandra township, Johannesburg, May 1986. Masked mourners are a common sight at funerals as people try to conceal their identities and protect themselves from the expected tear gas attacks.

The Muslim leader Moulana Faried Essack tries to stop police from removing an African National Congress flag draped over the coffin of slain ANC member Ashley Kriel in Langa township, Cape Town, July 1987. Symbols of the ANC, though illegal, are visible at funerals, an insistent reminder of the political meaning of the deaths. Although the ANC has been banned since 1961, it continues as a living presence and has the support of the majority of black people in South Africa.

Mourners at the funeral of a United Democratic Front activist shot by police join hands and sing in Guguletu township, Cape Town, 1986. Systematic shootings, police harassment, and detention without trial of key UDF figures have taken their toll.

**Inquests into the deaths of M. C. Miranda and S. Magmoet and
J. Claassen before Magistrate Mr. G. Hollman held at Wynberg,
December 1987**

*Although I was not working on 15 October 1985, I arrived home at
approximately 13h00. When I arrived there, Thornton Street was normal as it
was on every other day during the unrest period, but not normal as it was
before the unrest. Many children and people were milling around in the street
but there were no burning road barriers or stone throwing. At approximately
15h30, I noticed a burning road barrier in Thornton Street across from B.'s
shop. Many children and adults were standing on the pavement in front of
my house as well as on the corners of St. Simons and Thornton streets. I saw
these people and children messing with vehicles moving in the street. It
appeared to me as if they were stopping these vehicles. I went inside my
house and told A. A. to fetch our children at the madrassa [child care
center].*

*At approximately 16h00, A. returned with the children. The children
changed their clothes and went to play on the double couch in the lounge.
While they were playing, my son S. knocked on the door, and I opened it for
him. Thereafter, I. A. wanted to go home, but I told him not to do so. He did
not want to listen, so I opened the door for him and he went outside. G. R.,
S. M., E. R., S. R., I. R., S. R. and a woman called L. M. also went outside.
While they were going outside, I folded the washing lying on the double
couch.*

*I saw a yellow truck standing in front of my door and onion crates on the
back and persons dressed in khaki jump up from the crates. These people
dressed in khaki had guns and immediately started shooting in all directions.
I heard some of the bullets hit my house. I hid behind the open door and kept
it open for the children to return. While I kept the door open, the children
entered the house. S. M. fell in front of the door, holding his head, and
crawled into the house. I closed and locked the door. S. crept into the
bedroom which is located next to the lounge and partly lay down on the bed.
Thereafter, a big well-built man dressed in khaki entered the house and
grabbed I. R. who was hiding under the dressing table in the bedroom. G. R.
told him to leave I. alone. This man then grabbed S., who was half lying on
the bed and put him down at the step of the bedroom leading to the lounge.
A man dressed in blue arrived and spoke with A., who was holding her two
children. The big man dressed in khaki again grabbed S. and dragged him
into the living room. It seemed to me that S. was dead.*

Z. R.
from a signed affidavit, Legal Resources Centre

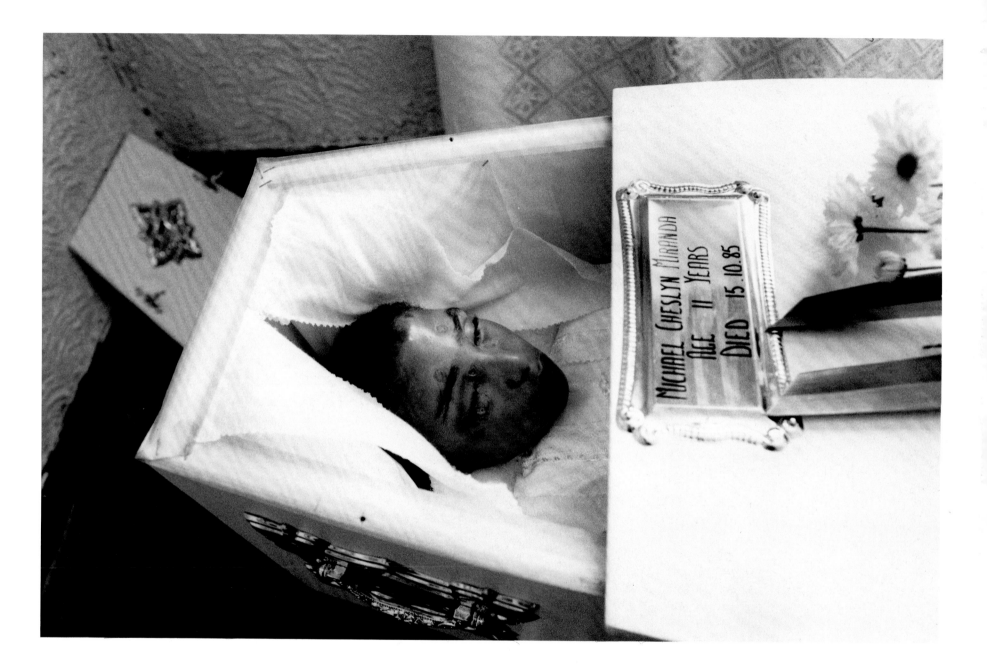

The body of Michael Cheslyn Miranda, eleven years old, lies in an open casket. Michael was one of three young boys shot by police in October 1985 in Athlone township, Cape Town, in what has become known as the ''Trojan Horse incident.'' The police had concealed themselves in wooden crates on the back of an open-bed railway truck that was driven twice down a residential street in Athlone township. A crowd of some 200 gathered as the truck made a second trip and threw stones at the vehicle. Springing from their hiding places, without warning, the police fired pump-action shotguns into the crowd. Michael Miranda died in the incident. Pathologists' reports revealed that Michael and another boy had been shot in the back. The worldwide horror at this and other brutal police actions in 1985 convinced the South African government to crack down on journalists and photographers who report such news.

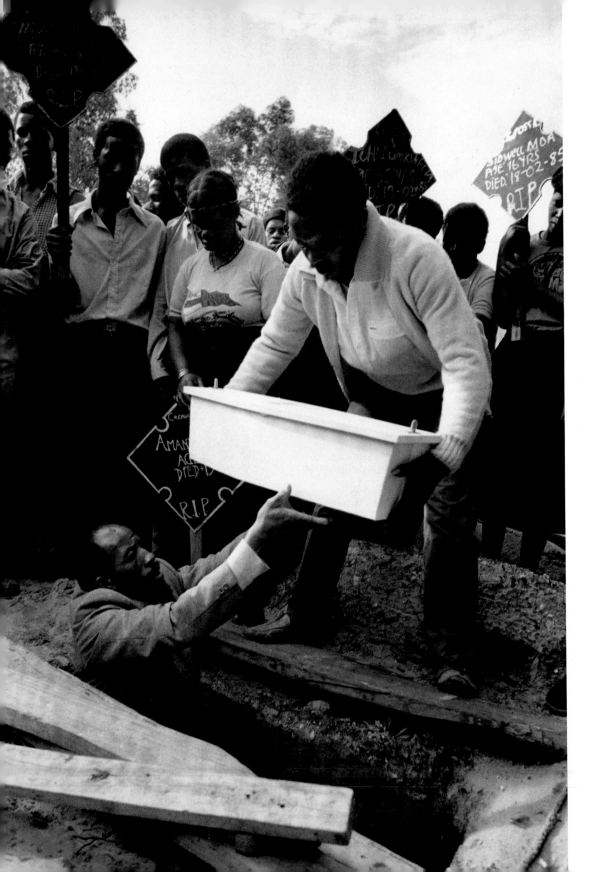

Left, Crossroads residents bury six-month-old Amanda Fanisa, asphyxiated by tear gas fired during police action, Crossroads, Cape Town, March 1985. Tear gas can be lethal, and it is especially dangerous when inhaled by young children. The South African security forces use tear gas as a standard means of "crowd control."

Opposite, coffins are lowered at the funeral of people killed in the "Queenstown massacre" when police opened fire after a meeting called to plan a consumer boycott, December 1985. In announcing the funeral, the United Democratic Front stated, "Through the blood of our comrades, a new South Africa will be born free from oppression and exploitation."

The Service Could Continue and Stop as Soon as Possible

In the course of the funeral at the stadium, the police arrived and surrounded the stadium with casspirs, hippos, etc., and were carrying rifles. I noticed that there was also a big police bus which stood in front of the entrance gate. The mourners and speakers ignored this high profile and presence of the police at the gate. I noticed that the crowd was increasingly getting restless. Suddenly there was a row at the entrance gate between the marshals and the police. When I looked there, I found that the police were physically forcing their way through and threatening to shoot the marshals there. The marshals were retreating inward. There was then disorder and chaos at the stadium as the crowd got restless. I, Rev. S. and B. M. went there and learnt from the marshals that the police had arrested one of the marshals. I cannot remember his name. We then tried to talk to the police. Rev. S. was actually speaking to the police who were in the yellow bus. We were raising our hands as a sign of peace and standing about 10 meters away from the said bus. These barbarians ignored us and, instead, prepared their rifles for shooting. I then started praying as I knew that these rascals would shoot us. They ignored us and instead drove the bus steadily away.

We then went back to the crowd, whereupon we met a contingent of other ministers who were also coming to address the police. As the yellow police bus had left the entrance gate, the priests and other leaders decided to go and see the station commander who was said to be at or near Archie Mbolikwa Higher Primary School, a black school near the mountain.

On their return, they reported to the mourners that the station commander had instructed that the service could continue and stop as soon as possible. This instruction was not only vague to us but was intimidatory and loaded with threat of possible police disruption of the service. We nevertheless continued but had to shelve off some of the speakers who were on the program. At the end of the funeral, we ensured that the mourners proceeded to the graveyard in a single procession. The priests walked right at the end of the procession. I was walking in front of the priests. The police had parked their vehicles all over the street, and some of them were wearing UDF, NEUSA and other T-shirts of peoples' organizations. I found this very strange. Near Nombulelo High School there was a yellow casspir and the yellow police bus, from which the police stood outside with rifles in their hands. These police shouted at the crowd, but I could not hear what they were saying, but I heard something like, "Kaffirs! [members of Bantu-speaking tribes; here used contemptuously] We are going to kill you today." They were not using the hailer [loud bullhorn for crowd control] but were all just shouting at us. They again got restless, and I, together with the priests, begged the crowd to ignore the police and proceed to the graveyard. We were about 15 meters away from the point turning to the graveyard when the police casspir/ hippo and the same yellow police bus came from behind towards us. I then sensed that something was going to happen. They drove past the priests, who were at the back but were near us, and a group of young boys, who were singing freedom songs. I, together with a certain B. M., then begged the boys to give way to the police so that they could drive past us. This B. M. had all along been playing a marshal role to these youths. The police had not gone past when they fired and hit Bigboy on the leg. He fell down, and the group ran away, dispersing in various directions. The police then went to B. M., who was lying down on the ground, and shot him for the second time. I cannot remember where exactly, but I think it was in the chest or the arm. The second shot was fired at a very close range of hardly a meter. B. M. was then dragged by the same white policeman who had shot him into the yellow bus like a bag of mielies. This was a very painful scene. It was as if my heart was bleeding from the inside, as I was looking helplessly and indignantly at B. M. being dragged by the white police towards their vehicle. The police then drove away. As they were driving away, I heard one of them (police) talking through a walky-talky or whatever, saying, "Ons het net nou 'n kaffir geskiet hier" [we have just shot a kaffir here]. I could not make out who he was talking to, but I imagined this was a superior or a station commander elsewhere.

N. J. S.
from Black Sash Archives

We Had Just Buried Our Children

The shooting started after the funeral of Michael Dirading on February 15. A security guard in a shop in Wynberg shot him. Thirteen thousand people went to Michael's funeral. I was one of them. We were washing at his home when the police arrived. The police fired tear smoke at us from their hippo [military vehicle]. Everyone ran, and then the police started going from yard to yard. The young people got ready to fight the police—first with stones and bricks, later with petrol bombs.

By four o'clock, Alexandra was a place at war. You heard endless gunshots. Above the township there was a heavy cloud of smoke from burning cars. A form 1 pupil was shot dead in front of her parents' home. Her death was just the beginning. I was trapped in a room with about 20 other people. Suddenly we were choking on tear smoke. A nine-year-old child with us fainted. We gave the child water and lit paper to get rid of the tear smoke.

Then I left. I was worried about my family, and I wanted to get home. As I crossed an open field, I saw a group of boys kneeling close together. I stopped them to tell them there was trouble, but when I saw what they were doing I wished that I hadn't stopped. The boys wore handkerchiefs over their faces.

They were making petrol bombs. I left as fast as possible. When I looked behind me, I saw a group of policemen. Suddenly, more boys started throwing stones at them. In the end, the policemen gave up and went back to their big "kwhela khwela" [police vehicle, used to convey prisoners].

When I saw more policemen coming, I went into the nearest house. The house stank of tear smoke and sweat. There were about 40 youths packed into the room. Three youths were lying on the floor, groaning in pain while another boy "operated" on them. He used a penknife and nail clippers to cut the flesh. He was taking either buckshot or bullets out of their legs. On Second, Third and Fourth avenues, I saw liquor running like water. Some boys had broken into the bottle-stores. Pensioners joined in; they forgot their troubles as they drank the free booze. But the youths didn't drink. They smashed liquor bottles for more than half an hour.

On Monday, the youths stopped the people from going to work. I was standing at Fourteenth Avenue. People were standing in their yards not knowing what to do. Suddenly there were some gunshots. M. T. fell. She was bleeding from her head. Then the streets of Alexandra turned into the "killing fields" of our times. Blood ran freely. Many people were wounded in the legs and body. First-aid teams moved about helping where they could.

On Wednesday, March 5, the people of Alex[andra] came together to bury the dead. They were joined by thousands of people from all over the country—and from all over the world. Under the cruel sun, the people of Alex[andra] listened to their leaders. The 17 coffins lay on a green carpet—guarded by young men in khaki uniforms. The coffins were wrapped in the colors of the African National Congress. Then the coffins were lifted shoulder high and carried to the cemetery. The dead were put to rest.

We slowly made our way home with heavy hearts. We had just buried our children, and we knew there would be more. But in our sadness we felt strong, too. We knew that our struggle does not stop here. It goes on. That is what our dead children would have wanted. We must make sure they did not die for nothing.

Anonymous
from *Learn and Teach*

Above, miners meet at the start of a national strike called by the National Union of Mineworkers (NUM) in Secunda, the Transvaal, August 1987. Gold mines led South Africa's industrial revolution, and minerals represent 70 percent of the country's current exports. Still, miners have yet to receive the most basic economic justice. With government support, mining companies control all aspects of miners' lives. Many miners are migrant workers from neighboring countries, forced to live in single-sex hostels near the mines. The companies and the government have tried to prevent miners from organizing, and the miners were the last to unionize in the 1970s. Because mine work is so closely linked to economic exploitation, the emergence of this union marks a new dimension in labor's resistance. Today, NUM is the largest union in the COSATU federation and has become a powerful force in the democratic political movement against oppression.

Right, Cosatu House, headquarters of the Congress of South African Trade Unions (COSATU), is occupied for five hours as po-
lice line up COSATU officials and search through their offices, April 1987. The police siege of Cosatu House followed a series of events linked to a union meeting in Germiston, a town some ten miles away. A massive railway workers strike was underway at the time, and the police violently disrupted a meeting in Germiston of the railway workers union. The police shot three workers, and a policeman suffered a fractured skull in the melee. Rumors reached Cosatu House that vigilantes had attacked the union meeting, and a group set off to help the workers in Germiston. Police intercepted these men, driving them back into the building. A black journalist, also assaulted and arrested during the siege, wrote, "I saw a badly injured and handcuffed man pushed down the stairs. After hitting the bottom of the stairs head first with a dull thud, he lay still. A young policeman moved up to him and hit him once on the ribs with a rubber 'pick handle.' The man didn't stir. He was dragged on the ground to a police truck before being thrown in head first" (*Weekly Mail,* 24–29 April 1987). A year later, an explosion destroyed Cosatu House.

Dairy workers march in solidarity with bakery workers on strike over wages and dismissals in Durban, June 1985. Durban was the birthplace of contemporary unionism in South Africa where workers' organizations have a long and important history. In the 1920s, the Industrial and Commercial Workers Union (ICU) organized black workers across the country, publicized flagrant injustices, and became the main focus for black resistance in the period from 1920 to 1930. During the early 1960s, the South African Congress of Trade Unions (SACTU) was active, and many African National Congress leaders engaged in trade union organization. When the government clamped down on black political and protest activities, SACTU was forced into exile along with the ANC in 1964.

Workers gather at a rally to launch the western Cape division of the Congress of South African Trade Unions (COSATU), Cape Town, February 1986. Founded in 1985, COSATU merged most of the black unions and is the largest federation of workers ever organized in South Africa. Despite government repression, COSATU survives. Its leaders have been detained without trial; its headquarters has been destroyed by bombs; and its local organizers assassinated. COSATU's leaders argue for the union's legitimate right as a representative trade union to address the political demands of its members, but the government has responded by attempting to outlaw the union's political activities. As a nonracial federation, COSATU also tries to win white workers to its ranks.

Police with bullhorns warn workers to disband. The South African government opposes black unions. In the early 1970s, the minister of labor remarked that black unions have "no necessity for existence." In the late 1970s, the government liberalized labor laws, allowing black unions to operate legally. This ushered in a period of worker organization and activism, leading to the formation of COSATU.

For Your Defence

Afrika!
Grow a big head
And
Sharpen your elbow.

Freedom

If the freedom I cry for
Is beneath the big Marula tree
I'll use my hands to dig it free.

OK Bazaars workers on strike meet at union headquarters in Cosatu House, Johannesburg, January 1987. A major supermarket chain, OK Bazaars has a large work force, organized by the Commercial, Catering, and Allied Workers Union (CCAWUSA), which has led many campaigns on behalf of food-store workers. The consumer power of black communities increases the strength of this union, and consumer boycotts have been effective in union efforts to improve labor conditions. The union's president is a young man, well known as a poet, and the two poems above were written by him.

Left, Florence Mkhize, a member of the Lamontville Education Crisis Committee (NECC), and a young student leader negotiate with officials of the Department of Education and Training over conditions in the schools, Durban, May 1986. During the period of school boycotts black education was severely disrupted. The educational system was seen as undesirable: textbooks distorted history, reflecting the government's view of the past; armed police patrolled school grounds and classrooms; and black education meant lower-grade industrial training. In the massive school boycotts of the mid-1980s, children and young people played a leading role in national politics. Democratic groups launched a new initiative for ''people's education'' at this time, establishing an alternative school system under popular control. NECC took the lead in these efforts. During 1987 and 1988, the government intervened, disrupting the program, detaining NECC leaders, and banning the organization. State education for blacks remains in crisis, with ''people's education'' a hope for the future.

Opposite, students at Lamontville High School protest against South African Defense Force attacks on African National Congress refugees in Zambia and Zimbabwe, Durban, May 1986. These students were not born when the ANC was banned. They were only toddlers when people in Durban celebrated the liberation of Mozambique in a famous meeting in 1974, a key event in the rekindling of political resistance in South Africa.

We Would Win Because We Were United

"We were very angry," said Gladman Jele, a worker at O.K. [a supermarket chain]. "In 1985 when we talked about increases, the O.K. bosses said that they could only give us R40. But they said if they made big profits, they would give us more money. We knew that the O.K. was making lots of money. Sometimes at the end of the day, the cashiers had to call people to help them count all the money they had taken. But we did not get an increase—we only got an extra half-day off."

"When we told the O.K. bosses last year that we wanted an R160 increase for everyone, the bosses said we were mad," Gladman went on. "They offered us R85 instead. But the bosses were playing with us—especially the people who have worked at the O.K. for a long time. People talked about a strike. So our union, the Commercial, Catering and Allied Workers Union of South Africa (CCAWUSA), organized all the workers to vote. All the CCAWUSA members at the O.K. voted for a strike. We knew before we started that we would win because we were united."

"It is easy to vote for a strike," said Isiah Thoka, another O.K. worker. "But to spend two months without pay is very difficult. I was lucky my brother is working. But everyone at home missed my wages. They all stood by me. They wanted us to win. So no one ever moaned because I wasn't bringing any money home. Other strikers had it tough. People couldn't pay their installments, and their furniture was taken away. Some people lost their houses because they couldn't pay the rent."

"In Jo'burg [Johannesburg], we came together every day. We met at Cosatu House, where our union offices are. We sang freedom songs. If there was a meeting with the O.K. bosses, the shop stewards came and told us what was said. Then we talked about it and decided what to do. We also got food from the union. The union bought food. Then some workers cooked it and sold it to us for fifty cents a plate. The money was used to buy more food for us. It was a great help."

"All this time, the Shop Stewards Council was very busy. They were making stickers and pamphlets for us to give out to people. We had to be very careful because of the Emergency laws. We could not say that people must boycott the O.K.—that is against the law. But we wanted people to know what was happening at the O.K. We wanted them to stop shopping there so that the bosses would agree to our demands. So we printed stickers that said, 'I don't buy from O.K.' We also took turns to picket outside the O.K. Every day people stood at the main doors of the O.K. shops with posters, telling people about the strike. The posters worked—the bosses did not like people knowing about the bad things that were happening there.'"

"The strike was difficult for CCAWUSA," Comrade Vivian Mtwa, general secretary of CCAWUSA, said. "It was the biggest strike we have ever had in CCAWUSA. The union did not have money to help so many people for such a long time. The O.K. bosses were also ready for the strike. They employed lots of casual workers to take the place of the strikers. All the meetings we had with the O.K. bosses ended with no agreement. The bosses did not want to know anything about the R160 increase. In the end we asked people to help us make an agreement. The O.K. bosses chose some people, and we chose some people. The meetings were hard work. Sometimes they went on through the night—until half-past five in the morning. 'In the end,' said Margaret Rathebe, 'we did not get everything we wanted. But we got more than the bosses first offered us.'"

from *Learn and Teach*

I Was Earning a Lower Wage Than That Dress

I don't remember the year, but I left my two kids at home and went to look for a job in Parktown. I left my children. I said to myself, "These children can talk, they can say 'I'm hungry' or 'I want to pee.' They are clever enough." So I left them with my granny and went to work.

I got a job as a domestic. I was there five years. The madam was nice, the master was nice. I liked the work. But I left because of my grandmother. She became ill, and I went to look after her. I took two weeks off. In the second week, my granny passed away. There was nobody to look after my kids. I started to panic. I started to look for a job where I could come home every night—factory work or something.

I struggled to find work. So I took some of my savings and went to an industrial school. You know, there's a school to learn sewing on industrial machines. I learnt how to use overlock, line stitch, buttonhole. I paid R25 for six months, and I learnt how to sew. It was in the sixties—there were ten of us in the class. We got jobs in a clothing factory. I started with overlock, waistline, and side seams.

I worked for many years—in three different clothing factories. I left my last job in 1980. This is what made me leave the job. They started to make funny ways of work—they were very strict with us. We had to make twenty-two dresses a day. They didn't care about the patterns. If it was a difficult pattern, we could only make three or four dresses a day. But they just wanted the work. If you couldn't make a large amount, they would shout at you and threaten to fire you. At that time I was earning R52.95 a week.

One Tuesday we were doing tennis dresses. You know, a tennis dress is a little thing like that. And those dresses cost R59 and some coins! Anyway, those dresses were wrong—the collar. They had come from another factory. The supervisor called me. She knew: Mabel is here, Mabel can fix it quickly. She piled all the dresses in front of me. The thing that made me mad was this. That dress was R59, and I was earning a lower wage than that dress! You know, if you were doing alterations, they used to take off the price tags. You mustn't see the price. But this time they forgot. I started to sew—two, three, four dresses. The supervisor asked me to hurry because they were waiting for the dresses.

Oh, I was cross. I said to the supervisor, "Come here. How much is this?" and I took out my pay slip. "And how much is this?" and I showed her the price tag. And I asked, "Do you want all these dresses this week?" She said yes. I said, "No, I'm leaving now." I didn't say anything. I just put my scissors, my tape—everything of mine—in a drawer and went out. Until today. It's already two years. I'm at home sewing and selling what I make. I won't work in a factory again.

Mabel
from *Working Woman*

You Find These Men by the Smell

Working in the mines is a painful thing. When you go down into the earth, you are not sure that you will come out alive. You don't want to think about it. But it keeps coming. When an accident happens, you think of your family. You become very lonely. You feel you want to see them for the last. Death will come to you some time. Death is so real you pray and thank God each time you come out alive. You work deep underground. Sometimes you work over three kilometers under the ground. The tunnel is dark. The heat makes the sweat run off your back.

Suddenly you hear a noise like thunder. The ground shakes. The rocks fall around you. Men run in every direction. Then it all stops. The men come back. They look for the dead and injured miners. The miners who can scream get help first. The others lie under the rocks for a long time. After four days you find these men by the smell.

an old miner
from *Learn and Teach*

The Story of One Tells the Struggle of All

Benoni, Boksburg, Springs, Egoli,
we make you rich.
We hostel people make you rich.
You send us back home to die with empty pockets,
empty dreams and dust in our lungs,
chopped-off hands and your machines grinding in our brain.

Benoni, Boksburg, Springs, Egoli,
we workers make you rich.
Dayshift, nightshift, overalls and sweat
keep the foundries pumping steel,
casting steel and costing money.

Don't worry brother, don't give up hope.
The sun shall rise for the workers.
Benoni, Boksburg, Springs, Egoli,
we shall make the people, all the people rich.

When you enter the hostel, you would not say it was a place where people live. You would think it was a place for pigs. Why? Because when we wake up in the morning, we cannot take a broom and sweep the place. We've got to go out to work. We have to start work at five o'clock in the morning. Often, there is no transport leaving Vosloorus at four o'clock. When you come back from work, you sweep the floors, you cook. After that, there is not time to sweep again. You go to sleep, you rise in the morning to go to work.

There are times when you can hardly sleep. The blackjacks raid the rooms looking for those who don't have permits to stay in the hostel. Like those people who are not employed, or those people who don't pay their bed fees. Now you can't sleep because the raids do not only wake these people. They wake up everybody.

Vosloorus Hostel is one of the many badly built and badly kept hostels which are part of our lives. They are small and cramped for so many people. The hard stone floors are cold in winter. The rooms have no ceilings. They are hot in summer. And the hostels are far from town. We are forced to work long hours and wait in queues for buses which often do not arrive. We came here to work for our families, but it is the white man who gets rich, and it is us who have done all the work. I know because I have seen this town grow. I have worked hard for twenty years but have nothing in my hands. The wealth we have created has been stolen by the bosses. They and their families are rich, but we have to live in hostels while our families suffer.

I found a job in the massive metal industries on the East Rand. The work in the foundry was hard and dangerous, and the hours were long. But I stuck out the tough and unsafe working conditions because there was no other place to go. We were the only people who could do this kind of work, and this was well known to our employers. Many of them knew migrant workers were the best workers. We were also prepared to do the heaviest of work. But they still treated us badly and still didn't treat us like human beings but like animals. They knew that as soon as they expelled us we would lose a place of residence, because we would not be able to pay the hostel fees without the money we earned. Then the pass office would be indifferent and instruct us to go back where we came from. That is very painful. But what is more painful is this. It is clear that profits mean more to the bosses than our lives. Our children could die in the countryside but they would still fire us.

from *The Sun Shall Rise for the Workers*

Above, striking workers at the British-owned BTR-Sarmcol plant use a play, *The Long March,* to tell their story, Durban 1986. The "father" of *The Long March* is a man named Zondi, a direct descendant of Bambatha, a chieftain who led a famous rebellion against colonial rule in 1906. Zondi has been active over the years in many political and worker organizations. The location of the play is Mpophomeni, a resettlement area where many BTR-Sarmcol workers live. In Zondi's version, the play explored the dispossession and forced removal of workers from their homes to Mpophomeni. Later, other worker groups changed the play's content, abbreviating the original history and focusing on current problems. In one version, for instance, a papier-mâché "Maggie Thatcher" mask highlights the "imperial factor" in the workers' struggle with a multinational company like BTR-Sarmcol.

Opposite, a delegation of women from the Food and Allied Workers Union participates in the Congress of South African Trade Unions' Culture Day, Johannesburg, July 1987. Theater is used for political expression. The women in Crossroads squatter town, for example, performed a well-received play, *Imfuduso,* dramatizing their long struggle to preserve their homes.

how do I tell this long tale?
that workers in my country march and fight
from within mines and factories
from within mealie-fields, fruit orchards and wheat fields
they march
from within despicable ghettoes and villages
from out the Bantustans and prisons
no longer with simplicity from ignorance
but they are simple of word
and so the little girls and boys
they emerge from out of an unripe youth
to mount the restless hour
they are freedom children.

Mongane Serote
from *A Tough Tale*

Workers turn actors in a play staged during Culture Day as part of the second national conference of the Congress of South African Trade Unions, Johannesburg, July 1987. In spite of severely repressive measures imposed by the State of Emergency, people have found ways to express their deepest feelings and ideas, creating new art forms like this "workers' play." In townships emerging nonracial forms of music, dance, and theater invigorate street and community life, giving force to ideas of liberation. To many participants and observers, the current cultural transformation of South Africa offers hope for a democratic, nonracial future "beyond the barricades."

A Sermon by a Local Parish Priest

We are gathered here today to mourn the provocation of Matola and the death of our brothers out there. The Lord no longer asks us to raise prayers to Him: He wants us to burst our chains. The dead have made their contribution. The task that remains faces those of us who are still alive. How do we continue our resistance? Each of us must regard himself as an apostle of resistance, and we must go all-out to recruit men and women who are ready to participate practically and actively in resisting oppression. We are in a situation where we are being forced, where we are being compelled by the sheer exercise of state violence, to think, not in New Testament terms, but in the Old Testament terms, where we speak of an "eye for an eye and a tooth for a tooth."

Violence has reached full circle. If the state thinks it has a moral right to use violence, why should the oppressed then not resort to violence as a viable means of changing the status quo? It seems that in this country we always speak with two languages: the white government speaks about "terrorists," but we shall always speak of "freedom fighters," and the deceased we are honoring today, we see as our martyrs. Amandla!

Crowd: *Ngawethu!*

Soweto civic leader: *For them, no linen for lining the coffin, nor carved casket do they lie in. No, strewn in their coffins, they lie with Makarov, with Scorpion, with Kalashnikov, with Umkhonto. Mayibuye!*

Crowd: *Afrika!*

Mother of one of the Matola dead: *Sons and daughters of the soil, our hearts are sore about what happened in Matola. Our boys were taken by surprise. I don't know what to call a man who does that.*

Crowd: *Coward!*

Mother: *Exactly! At night, when our boys suspected nothing, the cowards came in, well armed, to finish our poor children. And let me say that our children did not leave the country because of frustration or for some small reason—they left this country determined to return and get our country back. They are not terrorists, our children who died in Matola. Amandla!*

Crowd: *Ngawethu!*

Student leader: *The worst injustice which we can ever do to our comrades is to sit down and mourn and not take up their battle where they left off. Let our motto be: "We shall not mourn the dead," for if we concentrate on mourning, our eyes shall be clouded with tears, to an extent that we won't know where we are going, we won't be able to identify the enemy.*

What did our comrades die for? They died in pursuit of a better South Africa for us. They died in pursuit of a nonracial and democratic society. And they died for those principles enshrined in the most democratic document ever, the Freedom Charter. They left the country, they left the protection of their parents, the comfort of their homes, the warmth of their loved ones, and made the most supreme sacrifice in the human struggle. They said to themselves, "The struggle is my life," and they joined the people's army. Amandla!

Crowd: *Ngawethu!*

Student leader: *Now we have got to take up this fight and then try to mobilize the masses and educate them about those principles that the comrades died for. I shall request everybody to repeat after me these words which were their guiding principles, from the Freedom Charter. These freedoms . . .*

Crowd: *These freedoms . . .*

Student leader: *We shall fight for . . .*

Crowd: *We shall fight for . . .*

Student leader: *Side by side . . .*

Crowd: *Side by side . . .*

Student leader: *Throughout our lives . . .*

Crowd: *Throughout our lives . . .*

Student leader: *Until we win our liberty . . .*

Crowd: *Until we win our liberty . . .*

Student leader: *Power to the South African people! Education to the illiterate! And houses to the squatters! Mayibuye!*

Crowd: *Afrika!*

Matola Commemoration Service,
Soweto, February 22, 1981
from *South Africa: A Different Kind of War*

Masked youths raise the flag of the African National Congress at a rally marking the fourth anniversary of the United Democratic Front, Cape Town, 1987. After 1976, many ANC recruits were exiles from the Soweto uprising. Joining ANC's military wing, these young people sought military training, intending to prepare for a more effective struggle against the armed state. A new wave of militants has emerged from the conflicts of the mid-1980s. For the majority of people in South Africa, the ANC remains a positive symbol for liberation from poverty and oppression.

A Photograph Not Taken

If anybody reads this, I hope they can do something with it—or better still, something as a result of it. I am not a writer; I am a photographer. My work is about creating images for the news and other media. I feel compelled to communicate what I saw, in written form, because the general media restrictions have intervened in our work to an extent that it is almost impossible to operate.

On 5 December 1986, I attended a funeral in Mphophomeni, a Natal township, for four residents, trade unionists and students who had been assassinated by Inkatha. Even without the restrictions, I am not sure that this funeral would have hit the headlines. Maybe the "story" was not big enough to warrant full coverage.

On my way to the church in Mphophomeni, two roadblocks manned by the police and army informed us that photographs were strictly forbidden and that my equipment was not to leave my car. On arrival at the church, the presence of the only legal camera was very obvious. A police crew was busy videoing everybody at the funeral.

As the crowd of 700 waited for the coffins, there was an uncomfortable silence. The police and army presence was felt; you could read it on people's faces. There was none of the usual bravado, defiance and resistance we have come to expect from funerals in the last years. Instead, grief and pain abounded. There were no freedom songs, dancing or fiery speeches. We hung onto Archbishop Denis Hurley's careful words as he hailed the trade union movement and called for a commission of inquiry into these "savage and brutal murders by people we know."

A group of form-five pupils stood up to sing a song for a fallen comrade and classmate. Their farewell could not be completed as they broke down in hysterical wailing. A small procession carried his coffin out to be buried. Two crying children stumbled past, supported by the arms of a large mamma. Perhaps a photograph could have described beauty in a moment of such grief. Then we waited for the next coffin to be brought from the Pietermaritzburg police station. And the next. It was a very long funeral, interspersed with mournful hymns, and many silences. A shop steward got up to pay his respects to a long and close friend, but he broke down and couldn't finish. When the last coffin was buried, people gathered at the gravesite, surrounded by casspirs and gun-toting policemen.

For me this funeral represented the end of an era, and the beginning of another that will take all our courage to change. The invasion of our lives by those who stand for this government—be they Inkatha, vigilantes, the police and the army—make us as vulnerable as we all were in that church.

It was not by coincidence that this was the second funeral of an assassination I went to cover in a week. It is also not a coincidence that these immensely restrictive measures have been placed on the press. It should then come as no surprise that I ask to remain nameless and hope to hell people with this information can do something.

Anonymous

Who are they?

Moving in the park
I saw a notice nailed to the bench
'Europeans only'

Who are these Europeans
so fortunate to have seats
reserved for them
in Africa?

Walt oyiSipho ka Mtetwa

THE STATE OF EMERGENCY

On these three pages are included very brief excerpts from the Security Emergency Regulations. These regulations run into hundreds of pages in which new orders are issued and old orders are modified. This small sample of the orders conveys better than any description the nature and kinds of restrictions under which the South African people live. This selection has been compiled from issues of the *Government Gazette,* published by the South African Government.

PROCLAMATION BY THE STATE PRESIDENT OF THE REPUBLIC OF SOUTH AFRICA

Security Emergency Regulations (*Government Gazette* No. 11340)

Maintenance of order

2. (1) Whenever a member of a security force is of the opinion that the presence or conduct of any person or persons at any place in the Republic endangers or may endanger the safety of the public or the maintenance of public order, he shall in a loud voice in each of the official languages order such person or persons to proceed to a place indicated by him, or to desist from such conduct, and shall warn such person or persons that force will be used if the order is not obeyed immediately.

Arrest and detention of persons

3. (1) A member of a security force may, without warrant of arrest, arrest or cause to be arrested any person whose detention is, in the opinion of such member, necessary for the safety of the public or the maintenance of public order or for the termination of the state of emergency, and may under a written order signed by any member of a security force, detain or cause to be detained any such person in custody in a prison. . . .

(3) The Minister may, without notice to any person and without hearing any person, by notice signed by him and addressed to the head of a prison, order that a person arrested and detained in terms of subregulation (1), be further detained, and in that prison, for the period mentioned in the notice or for as long as these regulations remain in force. . . .

Power of entry, search and seizure

5. (1) If a member of a security force is of the opinion that it is necessary for the safety of the public, the maintenance of public order or the termination of the state of emergency, he may, without warrant but subject to subregulation (3)—
   (a) enter any premises, building, vehicle, vessel or aircraft and thereon or

therein take any steps which he is by a provision of these regulations or any other law authorized to take;
   (b) search any person or any premises, building, vehicle, vessel, or aircraft or any receptacle, object, or other article; or
   (c) seize any vehicle, vessel, or aircraft or any receptacle, object or other article. . . .

Restrictions on activities or acts of organizations

7. (1) If the Minister is of the opinion that it is necessary for the safety of the public, the maintenance of public order or the termination of the state of emergency, he may, without prior notice to any person and without hearing any person, issue an order by notice in the *Gazette* prohibiting an organization specified in the order, subject to subregulation (4) from carrying on or performing—
   (a) any activities or acts whatsoever
   (b) an activity or act specified in the order; or
   (c) activities or acts of a nature, class or kind specified in the order. . . .

Restrictions on activities or acts of natural persons

8. (1) If the Minister is of the opinion that it is necessary for the safety of the public, the maintenance of public order or the termination of the state of emergency, he may without prior notice to any person and without hearing any persons, issue an order under his hand whereby a person specified in the order is prohibited or is prohibited without the written consent of the Commissioner, from—
   (a) carrying on an activity or performing an act specified in the order
   (b) carrying on activities or performing acts of a nature, class, or kinds specified in the order;
   (c) being, at any time or during the hours specified in the order, outside the boundaries of an area likewise specified; or
   (d) being, during the hours specified in the order, outside the boundaries of the premises where he lives. . . .

Applications of certain provisions of the Prisons Act and Prison Regulations which are not otherwise applicable

(3) Notwithstanding the provisions as applied in terms of subregulations (1) and (2) to or in respect of a detainee, no detainee, shall be allowed under a power contained in those provisions to procure for himself from outside the prison any newspaper, foodstuff or potables, radio, record player, tape recorder, musical instrument or television set. . . .

Educational Institutions Emergency Regulations

Orders

2. (1) The Director-General may, for the purpose of the safety of the public, the maintenance of the public order or the termination of the state of emergency, and without prior notice to any person and without hearing any person, issue orders—

(a) whereby—

(i) the presence of a pupil on any school or hostel premises during such hours of the day as specified in the order or during weekends or public or school holidays;

(ii) the presence at any time of any other person on any school or hostel premises;

(iii) the participation by a pupil on any school or hostel premises in any activity specified in the order; or

(iv) the use of school property, facilities, equipment or accessories for a purpose or in connection with an activity specified in the order, is prohibited without authority of a person specified in the order or regulated or controlled in such other manner as may be so specififed;

(b) prohibiting the presentation on any school or hostel premises of any course or syllabus other than a course or syllabus contemplated in section 35 of the Education Act. . . .

(e) prohibiting the wearing, possession or displaying on any school or hostel premises of a uniform, part of a uniform, T-shirt or other article of clothing, case, flag, banner, pennant, poster, sticker, or any article on which—

(i) a slogan specified in the order or depicting support for any organization specified in the order or for any campaign, programme, project or action of such an organisation appears; or

(ii) the badge, emblem, name or flag of any organisation specified in the order appears; . . . .

Order Under the Security Emergency Regulations, 1988

Under the powers vested in me by regulation 7 of the Security Emergency Regulation, 1988, I, Adriaan Johannes Vlok, Minister of Law and Order, hereby prohibit the organisations specfied in the Schedule hereto, as from publication of this order and subject to regulation 7 (4) of the said regulations from carrying on or performing any activities or acts whatsoever.

Schedule:
Azanian People's Organisation
Azanian Youth Organisation
Cape Youth Congress
Committee for the Defence of Democracy
Cradock Residents Association
Detainees Parents' Support Committee
Detainees Support Committee
National Education Crisis Committee
National Education Union of South Africa
Port Elizabeth Black Civic Organisation
Release Mandela Campaign
South African National Students' Congress
South African Youth Congress
Soweto Civic Association
Soweto Youth Congress

Prohibition

2. The organisation known as Congress of South African Trade Unions is hereby, as from publication of this order and subject to regulation 7 (4) of the Security Emergency Regulations, 1988, prohibited from carrying on or performing activities or acts of the following nature, class, or kind, namely—

(a) the soliciting of support among members of the public or members of a section of the public. . . .

(b) the fomenting by way of publicity campaigns, of opposition among members of the public or members of a section of the public. . . .

(c) the making of calls on, or encouraging or inciting, members of the public or members of a section of the public by way of publicity campaigns to observe any particular day. . . .

(f) the making of calls or encouraging or inciting. . . .

(i) a person doing business in the Republic or with persons in the Republic, to disinvest from the Republic or to otherwise cease doing business in the Republic or with persons in the Republic.

(ii) the government of another country to institute or apply trade, economic or other punitive measures against the Republic or to sever or restrict diplomatic or other relations with the Republic; . . .

(iii) a person, organisation or body outside the Republic, to terminate, suspend or sever affiliations or ties with a person, organisation or body inside the Republic.

Media Emergency Regulations

In these regulations "subversive statement" means a statement—

(a) in which members of the public are incited or encouraged or which is calculated to have the effect of inciting or encouraging members of the public—

(i) to take part in an activity or to commit an act mentioned in paragraph (a), (b), or (c) of the definition of "unrest";

(ii) to resist or oppose a member of the Cabinet, or of a Ministers' Council, or another member of the Government or an official of the Republic or a member of the Government of a self-governing territory or a member of a security force in the exercise or performance by such a member or official of a power or function in terms of a provision of a regulation made under Public Safety Act 1953 . . .

(iii) to take part in a boycott action—

(aa) against a particular firm or against firms of a particular nature, class or kind, either by not making purchases at or doing other business with or making use of services rendered by that particular firm. . . .

(bb) against a particular product or article or against products or articles of a particular nature, class, or kind . . .

(cc) against a particular educational institution or against educational institutions of a particular nature, class or kind . . .

(iv) to take part in an act of civil disobedience—

(aa) by refusing to comply with a provision of, or requirement under, any law or by contravening such a provision or requirement; or

(bb) by refusing to comply with an obligation towards a local authority in respect of rent or a municipal service;

(v) to stay away from work or to strike in contravention of the provisions of any law, or to support such a stayaway action or strike;

(vi) to attend or take part in a restricted gathering. . . .

(x) to boycott or not take part in an election of members of a local authority or to commit any act whereby such an election is prevented, frustrated or impeded. . . .

"unrest" means—

(a) any gathering in contravention of an order under regulation 10

(1) (c) or (d) of the Security Emergency Regulations, 1988, or of a provision of another law . . .

(b) any physical attack by a group of persons on a security force or on a member of a security force or on a member of a local authority or on the house or family of a member of a security force or local authority; or

(c) any conduct which constitutes sedition, public violence, or a contravention of section 1 (1) (a) of the Intimidation Act, 1982 (Act 72 of 1982).

Presence of journalists etc., at unrest or security actions

2. (1) Subject to subregulation (2) no journalist, news reporter, news commentator, news correspondent, newspaper or magazine photographer, operator of a television or other camera or of any television, sound, film, or other recording equipment, person carrying or assisting in the conveyance for operation of such camera or equipment, or other person covering events for the purpose of gathering news material for the distribution or publication thereof in the Republic or elsewhere, shall, without the prior consent of the Commissioner or of a member of a security force who serves as a commissioned officer in that force, be at the scene of any unrest, restricted gathering or security action or at a place from where any unrest, restricted gathering or security action is within sight . . .

Publication of certain material prohibited

3. (1) Subject to subregulation (6) no person shall publish or cause to be published any publication, television recording, film recording or sound recording containing any news, comment, or advertisement on or in connection with—

(a) any security action . . .

(b) any deployment of a security force . . .

(c) any restricted gathering . . .

(d) any action, strike, or boycott by members of the public . . .

(f) any speech, statement or remark of a person . . . of whom it is commonly known that he is an office-bearer or spokesman of an organisation which is an unlawful organisation . . .

(g) the circumstances of, or treatment in, detention of a person . . .

(h) the release of a person who is detained. . . .

Taking of photographs, etc., of unrest or security actions

4. (1) No person shall without the prior consent of the commissioner or of a member of a security force serving as a commisssioned officer in that force take any photograph or make or produce any television recording, film recording, drawing or other depiction—

(a) of any unrest or security action or of any incident occurring in the course thereof, including the damaging or destruction of property or the injuring or killing of persons; or

(b) of any damaged or destroyed property or injured or dead persons or other visible signs of violence at the scene where unrest or security action is taking or has taken place or of any injuries sustained by any person in or during unrest or security action. . . .

(3) No person shall publish—

(a) a publication containing any photograph, drawing or other depiction; or

(b) a television, film, or sound recording, taken, made or produced in contravention of a provision of subregulation (1) or (2) of this regulation or of a provision of a regulation made under the Public Safety Act, 1953 (Act 3 of 1953) which was in force at any time during the period 12 June 1986 until immediately prior to the commencement of these regulations.

RESISTANCE, REFORM, AND REPRESSION IN SOUTH AFRICA IN THE 1980s

André Odendaal

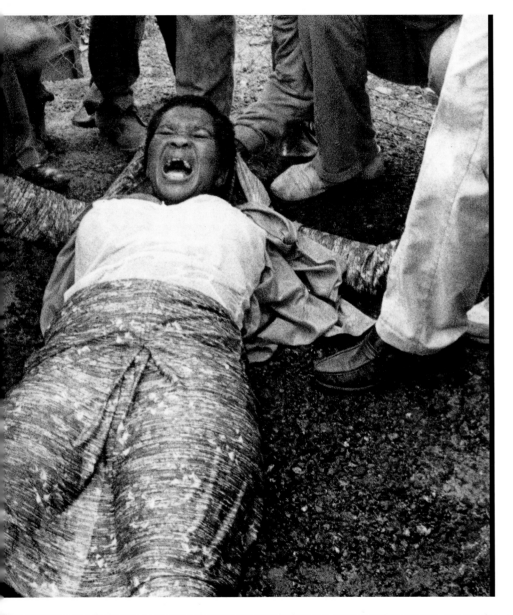

Sounds Like Firecrackers

When Caiphus Nyoka went to bed on the night of August 24, 1987, it was for the last time. At 4:30 the next morning his father, peeping through the living-room curtains of the family home, saw four policemen carry on a stretcher "the naked body of my son, lying faceup" to a waiting mortuary van. The 21-year-old anti-apartheid student activist had been shot in the forehead, neck, and chest at close range.

Two hours earlier armed policemen had hammered on the front and back doors of the Nyoka family's house in Daveyton, a black township near Johannesburg. When Abednego Nyoka, the father, opened the door of his house in Lemba Street, a uniformed white policeman pointed a rifle at him. The policeman's companions began to search the house.

Arriving at a room in the backyard that Caiphus Nyoka was sharing with three friends, the policeman kicked open the door, flashed lights into the faces of the young men, and demanded to know which one of them was Nyoka. When he identified himself, they ordered his friends to leave the room immediately.

In the yard outside, they were forced to lie facedown on the ground, dressed only in their underpants. From the room in which Nyoka remained with the policemen they now heard "sounds like firecrackers." Their clothes were thrown out, and they were told to dress quickly. Caiphus's father and sister, coming out of the house to investigate, were ordered back inside.

Handcuffed, the three friends were escorted at gunpoint to a white 10-seater minibus and driven to the Daveyton police station. Shortly after arriving there they saw a white policeman writing on a green blackboard. He told them to read what he had written. On the board were the words "999 Lemba Street—Caiphus Nyoka executed—Hands of Death." This policeman, slightly built, was dressed in jeans, a navy lumber jacket, and a balaclava, folded up above his eyes.

Responding later to reports of these events a police spokesman said, "Should the four have any complaints against the police, they are free to submit such complaints to the nearest police station." The nearest police station was that to which the three young men had been taken for their bizarre "reading lesson."[1]

Political resistance in South Africa today carries a high risk. The assassination of Caiphus Nyoka stands out only because it was carried out so openly. Murders of opponents of apartheid by mysterious death squads have become disturbingly commonplace. Mxenge, Goniwe, Ribeiro, Mntonga, Maake, September, Webster, and many others: the list is growing all the time.

These killings are symptoms of a conflict that has intensified dramatically over the past few years, particularly since September 1984, when the Botha government implemented a new constitution. Like the old, it was racially based. It totally excluded the African majority, though it provided a measure of representation for those Coloured and Indian people prepared to collaborate. Provoked by government intransigence posing as reform, and by living conditions made intolerable by economic hard times, black anger boiled over. In the township ghettoes where black people are forced to live, residents came out in open revolt against apartheid. The scale of revolt soon outpaced the fury of the 1976 Soweto uprisings, which had drawn worldwide attention. For more than a year the streets of the townships were open battlegrounds. Pushed beyond despair the inhabitants defended their humanity with stones and anything else that came to hand against the tear gas, bullets, and armored vehicles of the besieging army and police. Newspapers provided daily "unrest charts," weather maps that charted the course of the political hurricane.

The world looked on as the apartheid regime responded with ever-increasing brutality. The townships were occupied by the army and police. Opponents of apartheid were harassed, detained, and killed. Since 1984 an estimated 3,500 people have died in South Africa. As many as 55,000 have been detained. A high proportion of these have been children. During 1986 alone, 8,800 children were held, some no more than nine years old. Four States of Emergency, each more severe than the last, gave the security forces Draconian powers. South Africa is now virtually under martial law. The security forces have almost unlimited powers and indemnity from prosecution. The courts are powerless to intervene. Indeed they are often seen to be upholding apartheid laws. Newspapers are gagged by strict censorship. Opposition to apartheid has been virtually outlawed. Meetings are banned. Political leaders have been silenced through bannings, jail, and exile. In restrictions announced in Februrary 1988, seventeen organizations were prohibited "from carrying on, or performing, any acts whatsoever." When the churches, one of the few channels left for opposition, tried to petition Parliament in protest, church leaders—including Archbishop Desmond Tutu—were arrested. Later the headquarters of church groups were mysteriously bombed.

The state has now quelled the most visible manifestations of the revolt that broke out in 1984, and crippling restrictions on the media have removed South Africa from the glare of international publicity. Yet behind the blanket of censorship, the deadly struggle between the forces of repression and the forces of liberation continues. Not a day passes without violence. As a state devoid of moral and political legitimacy resorts more and more to naked repression, darkness is descending over the land.

The images presented here have been selected from the work of twenty South African photographers who documented the crisis day by day and street by street. As the conflict unfolds, the stress lines show up through the lens of the camera. Sometimes these are present on individual human faces—taut with anger, masked by grief or death, looking down over the steel sides of a troop carrier or up from the polished wood of a coffin. Sometimes, as in the cover photograph, the eyes of the combatants seem to meet. More often they are caught up in a field of force that impels them blindly, steel and muscle against sinew and stone, mists of tear gas swirling around the flaming barricades. Or it is tableau against tableau, the stage play of power against the street theater of resistance, the fancy dress of re-

form against the impromptu dance of a new culture in the making. Nadine Gordimer has commented that photography has become the most emotive language of the several dozen spoken by us South Africans. These pictures show why.

Three Centuries of Violent Rule

The present State of Emergency is the outcome of more than three centuries of violent rule by the white minority over the black majority. As the leading anti-apartheid body, the African National Congress (ANC) points out:

> South Africa was conquered by force and is today ruled by force. At moments when white autocracy feels itself threatened, it does not hesitate to use the gun. When the gun is not in use legal and administrative terror, fear, social and economic pressures, complacency and confusion generated by propaganda and "education" are the devices brought into play in an attempt to harness people's opposition. Behind these devices hovers force. Whether in reserve or in actual employment, force is ever present and this has been so since the white man came to Africa.[2]

European colonists arrived in 1652 and at first used force to conquer African societies and to dispossess the indigenous people of their land. But since the late nineteenth century—when the process of conquest was completed and modern, industrial South Africa began to develop following the discovery of the world's richest mineral resources—coercion has ensured a constant supply of cheap black labor to facilitate the creation of wealth for local (white) and international capital.

The modern apartheid system emerged from this history of colonial conquest and the exploitation of African labor. Africans, 80 percent of the population, were segregated into reserves—the so-called *Bantustans*, or homelands—constituting only 13 percent of their former land. More than 300 laws were put on the statute book to control their lives from the cradle to the grave. Africans were allowed into the "white" areas only as "labor units," housed usually in ghetto settlements or single-sex hostels, and expected to return to the reserves and their families after completing their contracts. Rigid control of black settlement, movement, and labor—these have been the main objects of the apartheid system, and they underpin the racial discrimination, political domination, segregation, migrant labor, Bantustans, forced removals, repression, and gross inequalities in wealth found in South Africa.

The pass laws, which prescribed where blacks could work, live, and travel, formed the basis of this system of control. Until 1986, when more subtle forms of influx control replaced these laws, all Africans had to carry passbooks, like badges of slavery. They suffered daily harassment. In the seventy years of the pass laws, an estimated 16.5 million blacks were arrested, psychologically humiliated, and criminalized for contravening them.

For more than a hundred years a migrant labor force has underpinned the South African economy. One in three workers is a migrant laborer—those "labor units" having no permanent residence rights. More than 2 million workers come to the cities each year on contract. Another 600,000 people commute daily from the rural Bantustans to the "white" cities. As many as 20 percent of these workers—the "night riders"—travel 3.5 to 7 hours per day, snatching a few hours' sleep at home before boarding the buses again.

The apartheid planners thought that the Bantustans could be self-sustaining. However, the production systems there have long since collapsed. Most income is derived from money sent back from the cities by migrant workers. Poverty is endemic. About a quarter of rural males are more than 20 percent underweight. The infant mortality rate is at least one in four. A study of 2,609 schoolchildren in a rural community in the eastern Transvaal showed that 39 percent of them had no breakfast before coming to school, 16 percent were suffering from bilharzia, and 46 percent from active tuberculosis. An average of 706 people shared one water tap.

The urban townships are not much better. They are poor, ugly, and overcrowded. A 1985 National Building Research Institute report found 7.4 million black township residents living in only 466,000 "relatively small" housing units (an average of nearly 16 persons per dwelling). Most townships lack electricity and other essential amenities. For instance, Langa near Cape Town has no children's playgound, no post office, no pharmacy, no public library, no dentist, and no internal railway link.

According to internationally accepted measurements, South Africa has "the unenviable distinction of having the most unequal distribution of income for any economy for which data is currently available." While the living standards of South African white are equal to any in the first world, half of all African households in the country live below the "least generously drawn poverty line."[3]

Roots of the Present Conflict: Soweto and "Reform"

Apartheid became state policy in South Africa when the present National party government came to power in 1948. The Nationalists sowed a mine field of laws affecting every area of life and implemented the apartheid policy ruthlessly. Within two decades, for instance, they forcibly relocated over 3 million black people to fit in with their chessboard designs. When black opposition movements rose in protest, they were banned and driven underground. By 1970, white rule seemed on the surface to be absolute, apartheid unshakeable. Not only were the small white minority running the country with an iron hand, they were also better off than ever before. During the 1960s, the greatest economic boom in the country's history, resulting in a growth rate equaled only by Japan, had bought them what one commentator called "a careless affluence rivaling that of Californians." The American magazine *Fortune* could conclude that "South Africa is one of those rare and refreshing places where profits are great and problems are small. Capital is not threatened by political instability or nationalization. Labor is cheap, the market booming, the currency hard. . . ."[4]

Yet a few years later South Africa was in revolt. On June 16, 1976, Soweto students took to the streets to protest against a government directive that Afrikaans be used as a language of instruction in black schools. The protests grabbed world headlines as they turned into a general uprising that spread to most other parts of the country. The current crisis in South Africa has its roots in those transition years in the 1970s.

The 1976 uprising was precipitated by a number of developments, economic, political, and military, which had a lasting effect on South African politics. Following the worldwide recession that accompanied the Middle East war and the OPEC oil price hikes in the early 1970s, the South African economy entered a sustained period of crisis and recession, which has been relieved only periodically since then by short upturns made possible by rises in the price of the country's main commodity, gold. The recession brought unemployment and inflation. The government's refusal to recognize the permanency of the ever-increasing urban African population caused poor township conditions. Wages were at a poverty level. These conditions, coupled with the lack of avenues for the expression of black views, led to a dramatic growth of black militancy and organization.

The repressive calm of the 1960s was broken as workers throughout the country began to organize and make demands. Their actions led to the emergence of a mass-based democratic trade union movement, which by the end of the 1970s had become a significant force in South African politics. The militant black consciousness movement provided another front of popular struggle. Black consciousness called on blacks to free themselves psychologically from dominant Eurocentric values, and to be assertive and proud of their cultural heritage instead of cooperating in their own oppression. Then, successful struggles for independence in the neighboring countries of Mozambique and Angola (and later Zimbabwe) led to the collapse of colonial rule in those countries. The African revolution had arrived at the very borders of the white South and infused the black masses with a sense of their own potential.

The pressures described above set in motion a process that continues today. Slowly but surely the balance of power altered in favor of the oppressed black majority. Minority rule in South Africa entered a deep-seated structural crisis. Existing institutions no longer resolved the strains and contradictions within South African society. The Soweto uprisings shattered the myth of white invincibility and made it impossible for the white minority to continue to rule in the old way, thus setting the scene for the politics of the 1980s.

The state—via the police—responded to the Soweto uprisings by killing nearly one thousand people during 1976/1977. In October 1977 the government banned eighteen organizations and closed down a black newspaper. The black consciousness movement leader Steve Biko was murdered in detention, causing an international outcry.

Putting down the revolt could not hide the crisis. It was clear that the clinical segregation of the races envisaged under apartheid was a pipe dream. The government, therefore, began in the late 1970s to seek ways of restructuring and modernizing its policies and institutions. The prime minister warned that white South Africans would have to "adapt or die." "Reform" became the new key word.

Government reform focused on broadening the base of political and economic privilege to ensure stability—without endangering white hegemony. A minority of blacks were offered a stake in the apartheid system. Simultaneously the government tightened administrative and military controls over the majority. The aim of "reform" was not to do away with apartheid, only to make it more workable.

The government focused on four main areas. It set about devising new political institutions, local and central. It reorganized the security management system. It revised its industrial relations system by "legalizing" the hitherto independent trade unions and trying to incorporate them into the official industrial relations process. Finally, it changed urban policy, easing certain influx control restrictions on a favored group of urban Africans, the so-called "insiders"—people who had lived "legally" in towns for ten years. They were promised better housing, secure tenure, and even property ownership. At the same time, however, influx control over the mass of "disqualified" Africans, or migrants, was tightened, and thousands were driven out of the cities back to the impoverished rural homelands.

The government wished to create a stable black urban middle class and a relatively privileged stratum of workers—divided from the mass of rural Africans and migrants—who would be ready to strike a bargain with state and business. This was the purpose of "reform." The Afrikaner Nationalist government was attempting to broaden its narrow ethnic power base by co-opting English-controlled big business and a black elite into a new multiracial ruling-class alliance. In this way the white-minority government hoped to stave off the demands of the mass of blacks for full political rights in an undivided South Africa.

Military leaders and the English-speaking big business establishment played a significant role in the government's reform program. Departing from the practice of appointing career politicians to top government posts, Prime Minister Botha promoted the head of the South African Defense Force, General Magnus Malan, to the cabinet and gave the State Security Council (SSC) the status of a "second cabinet." Consisting of senior cabinet ministers, heads of some state departments, and leaders of the defense force and police, the SSC was to monitor security matters and the general administration of the state. Today, the SSC acts effectively as "a shadow government." Observers who warned in the 1970s about "a creeping military coup" have been proven correct. The military managed much of the reform process and, in tandem with the Nationalists, elaborated a national security ideology. This emphasized that South Africa was facing a "total onslaught" by the forces of "international communism" and its allies, including the black liberation forces and even the Western media. A "total strategy" was required in reply. The battle was over hearts and minds. All sectors of the population—including business, the press, and other institutions—had to be harnessed in support of this total strategy. If you are not with us, you are against us, the reasoning went. Thus the government was given a free rein to proceed with changes while simultaneously tightening its grip on opponents. As a recent study has noted, "reform has to be understood in terms of how the white minority has defined its security interests, reshaped the security system and co-ordinated the whole state bureaucracy to deal with any conceivable threat to its interest."[5]

South African big business was closely involved in the apartheid reform process. Leading industrialists joined the Defense Advisory Board, which is responsible for injecting new business techniques into the South African Defense Force. More than one thousand companies became associated with the activities of the parastatal Armscor corporation, which was formed to circumvent the arms boycott of South Africa and has now matured into an arms-exporting military-industrial complex worth billions of rand. Conferences between Prime Minister Botha and the country's business leaders in 1979 and 1981 confirmed the cosy relationship existing between them. Most business leaders publicly endorsed the government's plans in a referendum called to test white opinion in 1983.

After Soweto, big business became uncomfortably aware that black opposition went deeper than explicit protests against racially discriminatory apartheid measures. Blacks were challenging the whole economic system based on cheap black labor underpinning apartheid. Business responded by launching the Urban Foundation, a massive project aimed at improving conditions in black townships and softening attitudes toward capitalism. A memorandum by the Federated Chamber of Industries to the prime minister showed how much the ideas of the apartheid government and business were coinciding. It declared that only by having the urban black middle class "on our side" would white South Africa be assured of containing "the irresponsible economic and political ambitions of those blacks who are influenced against their real interests from within and without our borders."[6]

Business has benefited greatly from government reform. In the 1980s, the government added the catch phrase of "free enterprise" to that of "reform." Increasingly it is unfettering the private sector from existing restrictions in the hope that this will provide the economic growth necessary to ensure political stability. In a country where blacks have only a minimal stake in the economy, this means more and more wealth is being concentrated in fewer and fewer (white) hands. As it is, a mere five companies own 80 percent of the Johannesburg stock exchange. The National party is today no longer so much the party of Afrikaner nationalism, as the party of unrestricted free enterprise and militarism.

The government released a new constitution setting out its plans for political reform in 1983. The constitution provided for a new tricameral Parliament with separate chambers for Coloureds, Indians, and whites, and a new executive state president enjoying far-reaching powers. A departure from the old Westminister-style system, the new constitution was nevertheless still firmly grounded in apartheid ideology. Legislation was to be dealt with by the three racial chambers separately. If they could not agree on a new law, a President's Council would make the final decision. In both the council and the electoral college that elected the president, whites were guaranteed majorities. This ensured that the junior black partners would never be able to force through dissenting decisions. The powerful president could dissolve Parliament, declare war, and appoint ministers from outside Parliament. The post was tailor-made for P. W. Botha: he would have the power to repress black revolt on the one hand and on the other to push through limited reform from above against the wishes of *verkrampte* (ultraconservative) whites. This strategy of simultaneous repression and reform was at the heart of the Botha modernization program.

What about the Africans, who comprised four fifths of the population? The constitution completely excluded them. In fact, it mentioned them only once. Clause 93 declared, "The control and administration of Black affairs shall be vested in the President. . . ." According to the logic of apartheid, Africans were not part of South Africa and had to find their political homes in the ethnic Bantustans governed by often ruthless and corrupt allies of the government. The government hoped to get rid of the "black problem" by giving the various homelands independence (thereby turning South Africans into foreigners in the land of their birth). Outside the Bantustans, however, millions of Africans had permanently settled in the urban areas of "white" South Africa. Acknowledging that these urban Africans existed, the government introduced the so-called Koornhof bills in 1982 to put black local government on a new footing. The bills defined who could live and work in the urban areas, tightened controls in the townships, and designed a system of local authorities staffed by blacks. Town councils were given greater administrative and police powers than before. As the townships lacked any commercial or industrial base for providing revenue, residents were to pay for the new township bureaucracies by means of higher rents and other taxes. The Koornhof bills directly complemented the new constitutional proposals. Indeed, as critics pointed out, the bills were "the most far-reaching and devastating element of the reform package." They confirmed the exclusion of Africans from power and laid down tight controls over them.

Overall the so-called reform package did not constitute reform at all. Rather, it streamlined political domination and control. "Reform" was an attempt by the apartheid government to contain the political aspirations of the millions of South Africans who remained excluded from the vote.

Now Is the Time: Anti-Apartheid Struggles after Soweto

On November 2, 1983, a whites-only referendum endorsed the new constitution. In response, popular organizations took up the cry:

> *We want all our rights,*
> *We want them here (in a united South Africa)*
> *And we want them now . . .*
> *Now is the time!*

Black South Africans showed clearly that they had not been fooled by the state's sham reforms. From the late 1970s onward, a growing militancy was organized on three main fronts: the expanding trade union movement, the armed rebellion of the banned African National Congress, and the reemergence of legal, mass-based political movements. These different strands of resistance became increasingly interlinked in the 1980s.

Perhaps the most significant feature of black politics in the post-Soweto era was the rapid growth of the trade unions that had emerged from the labor unrest of the early 1970s. Black union membership jumped from 40,000 in 1975 to 247,000 in 1981 and to 1.5 million in 1985. The independent unions astutely countered attempts to weaken their power. From 1981, they embarked on unity talks aimed at creating a national federation to represent working-class interests. The result was the launching in 1985 of the Congress of South African Trade Unions (COSATU), representing the nonracial trade unions, and the formation the following year of the National Council of Trade Unions (NACTU), a similar, but smaller federation with black consciousness and Africanist orientations. Today, both NACTU and, in particular, COSATU are key actors on the South African political stage.

The intensification of the armed struggle of the banned ANC was another important feature of politics after Soweto. The ANC reemerged as the main political force in the struggle against apartheid. Formed in 1912, one year before the founding of the currently ruling National Party, the ANC claimed a membership of 100,000 by 1960. Then it was banned and forced underground, beginning the armed struggle against white minority rule. After 1976, thousands of fleeing students crossed the borders to join the movement and undergo military training. "Soweto's youth has disappeared," the *World* newspaper (soon to be banned) commented in response to low school attendance figures after the uprising. Revitalized by this influx, the ANC began to strike with increasing effect at targets within the country. By 1982, the minister of justice admitted that "the ANC is everywhere." At the same time, ANC prestige was increased by an ideological reorientation within the broad resistance movement. Black consciousness, the dominant tendency in the early 1970s, was now supplanted by a more broad-based, nonracially motivated struggle giving more weight to the economic (rather than simply racial) basis of oppression, and thus of apartheid, in South Africa. Most supporters of this line backed the Freedom Charter, the guiding document of the ANC adopted in 1955, as a basic program for struggle.

The anti-apartheid struggle after 1978 also gained strength from the emergence of a new generation of community-directed, "first-level" (grass-roots) organizations. These groups sought to redress the lack of effective organization among the popular forces, deficiencies that had been exposed by the spontaneous, undirected nature of the 1976–1977 uprisings, and the internecine conflict that had sometimes occurred as a result (for instance, between students and workers). The new community groups began by concentrating on specific bread-and-butter issues. Their names were suggestive: the Joint Rent Action Committee, Driefontein Residents

Committee, Joint Commuters Committee, Cape Action Housing Committee, Natal Anti-SAIC Committee (to oppose elections for the puppet South African Indian Council), Port Elizabeth Black Civic Organization, United Women's Organization, Congress of South African Students, Detainees Parents Support Committee, Release Mandela Committee, and others.

These grass-roots groups organized successful boycotts, marches, and demonstrations, establishing a solid basis for the fierce resistance of the 1980s. Political leaders hoped to build from this basis "progressively more political forms of organization," which would culminate in a national struggle through a "more or less coherent national democratic movement." Soon these hopes were being fulfilled. Community groups led campaigns to boycott products of firms whose workers went on strike. During school boycotts in 1980, students worked closely with the community groups. Similarly, ANC units sabotaged electricity substations supplying white areas in Durban after the municipal authorities had responded to a community campaign against increased electricity charges by cutting off supplies.

National campaigns followed. The first was coordinated against the celebration of the twentieth anniversary of Republic Day (the day on which the white Republic was founded) in 1981. Then a wide range of groups, including student organizations, the Release Mandela Committee, and a number of trade unions, participated in a successful national campaign against the elections for the impotent South African Indian Council in November of the same year. A new unity was emerging. When the government spelled out plans for its new constitutional dispensation in 1982, opposition forces again answered with a single voice. But now, in addition to the usual call for an ad hoc front to oppose the Botha regime's blueprint for the future, calls were made for more concrete cooperation.

On January 9, 1983, the president of the World Alliance of Reformed Churches, Dr. Allan Boesak, called on churches, civic associations, trade unions, student organizations, and sports bodies to form a front to fight the government's proposals. Boesak's speech was the catalyst for the launch of the United Democratic Front (UDF) on August 21 at Mitchells Plain, near Cape Town, where the white Parliament was in session. Among the 12,000 who attended were 2,000 delegates from 320 organizations claiming to represent over 1 million people. One black newspaper heralded the event as "a new phase in the struggle for liberation in South Africa." Dr. Boesak contended that this was "the birth of what could become the greatest and most significant people's movement in more than a quarter of a century." The government and its media ignored the UDF launch, focusing instead on a rugby writers conference aimed at breaking South Africa's sporting isolation.

The formation of the UDF highlighted the continuity between past and present struggles. Although it was illegal to identify openly with the ANC or propagate armed struggle, the UDF stressed that it shared the broad aims espoused by the ANC when that body was still legal. The UDF opened up a new front in the struggle that would complement and not, it emphasized, supersede the struggle of the respected exile movement. Nelson Mandela and the other ANC leaders, incarcerated for more than twenty years in maximum prisons on Robben Island and elsewhere, were made patrons of the UDF. The UDF also appropriated many songs, slogans, and symbols from the 1950s.

Although efforts were made to create the broadest possible anti-apartheid front, not all the opposition groups joined the UDF. Adherents of the black consciousness philosophy formed the National Forum Committee, which opposed the involvement of anti-apartheid whites, rejected the Freedom Charter, and emphasized anti-capitalist over anti-apartheid aims. The Azanian People's Organization (AZAPO) was the most important affiliate of this body. The UDF and the National Forum Committee organized side by side with the same broad aims, their relationship tense and at times antagonistic as a result of ideological and organizational strains (and, later, the work of *agents provocateurs* operating on behalf of the apartheid system).

Initially the trade unions also shied away from uniting openly with the political organizations. Unions feared that state repression of "political" activity would invite retaliation that subverted workers' gains. They believed a union's function of addressing shop-floor issues was weakened by political activism, and that the union's principle of democratic accountability to its members would be difficult to maintain within a less structural alliance such as the UDF.

The UDF and National Forum Committee drew a distinction between the progressive forces and black groups that participated in the apartheid system. Those who supported the new tricameral Parliament, unrepresentative urban local councils, and the ethnically based homeland system were isolated from opponents of the regime. Among those shunned was Chief Gatsha Buthelezi of KwaZulu, and his Inkatha movement. Using the protection offered to those working within the apartheid system, and the powers of patronage a Bantustan "homeland" has at its disposal, Buthelezi has built a powerful base and set himself up as a "third force" in opposition politics. By refusing independence, offering limited opposition to the government, and espousing "moderate" policies—including a retreat from the demand for one person one vote—he seeks to be the kind of alternative to apartheid that the white business community and conservative Western leaders would support. With the tacit approval of the state, Inkatha has attempted to undermine organizations like the UDF, the ANC, and the progressive trade unions—for example, by establishing a rival body to the latter—and it has engaged in violent confrontations with these groups.

The major challenge for the UDF was to succeed in its stated aim of opposing the government's "new deal." The UDF soon attracted widespread support. It first successfully coordinated a boycott of local government elections for the Coloured and African communities. The 10 percent turnout thoroughly discredited from the start the government's new structures for governing urban Africans as outlined in the Koornhof bills. The UDF then began a campaign to collect 1 million signatures against the ratification of the constitution. Thousands of volunteers went door to door urging people, in the words of the campaign slogan, to "Make Your Mark Against Apartheid." The aim was not only to voice opposition to the constitution, but also to mobilize support and build organization. Big rallies where people of all races demonstrated their commitment to nonracialism drove home forcefully the UDF's guiding message: "Apartheid Divides, UDF Unites." UDF's first birthday rallies in August 1984 coincided with the eve of the elections for the new tricameral Coloured and Indian houses. "Don't Vote" was the unequivocal call. Guarded by police, who engaged in running battles with protesters, only 18 percent of the registered Indian and 21 percent of the registered Coloured voters turned up on polling day. Many more who were eligible had not bothered to register. Almost 1 million students at schools and universities boycotted classes to protest the new deal.

The polls were a clear rejection of apartheid's sham reforms. One London newspaper declared that the message was clear: "the aircraft has crashed and it is necessary to go back to the drawing board." Dr. Allan Boesak, whose call for unity had led to the formation of the UDF, warned that if the government proceeded with its constitution new unrest and tensions would be created. Soon, the warning was realized.

Insurrection, 1984–1986

On September 3, 1984, the tricameral system and the executive state president were inducted with pomp and ceremony. On the same day, rioting erupted in the Vaal triangle. Angry crowds took to the streets. They killed government collaborators stoned vehicles, burned government buildings and cars, and looted shops and businesses (many owned by corrupt councilors). Newspapers reported this the "bloodiest day" since Soweto in 1976.

The Vaal uprisings, as they became known, ushered in a new phase of militancy and resistance in South Africa. Over the next few months urban insurrection became endemic. Spontaneous street clashes between township residents and the security forces superseded the organizational forms of response established by the UDF over the past year. Existing UDF structures could no longer control or keep pace with the rapid mobilization and politicization that occurred. Militant youths, armed with no more than stones and petrol bombs, embarked on a crude guerrilla struggle against well-armed government forces. Soon state authority collapsed completely. Three months into 1985, as one analyst noted, few would have disputed that South Africa was in the grips of a low-intensity war.

The township insurrections were linked broadly to the political exclusion of the African majority. But the immediate causes of strife were the economic hardships induced by a recession dating from 1982 and the illegitimacy of the new local authorities' structures. In Sebokeng, the epicenter of the uprisings of September 1984, at least a quarter of the households lived below the poverty line. When the new government-sponsored local councils imposed rent and other increases to subsidize their operation, the people took to the streets. *Asinamali*—we have no mo-

ney—was the banner behind which they marched. Economic grievances meshed easily with political ones.

The hurricane raged from region to region, eventually touching every corner of South Africa. From its source in the southern Transvaal—the industrial heartland of South Africa—the mass unrest swirled over into the northern Orange Free State and down to the eastern Cape in the new year. Later in 1985, the other major urban and industrial areas, Cape Town and Durban, as well as the rural northern Transvaal became major sites of struggle.

The most lasting impressions of this period of revolt were the David-and-Goliath street clashes between township residents and the army and police—unforgettable scenes were beamed into millions of homes around the world. However, beneath the surface of open revolt, other important forms of struggle included massive worker stay-aways, and rent, consumer, and school boycotts. Within two years, some 300,000 households in 53 townships throughout the country were refusing to pay the rents demanded by the unpopular new government councils. By refusing to "subsidize their own oppression," the residents denied the councils the legitimacy they sought and cost the state dearly—an estimated 500 million rand by late 1986. Similarly, black schoolchildren crippled the black education system, a source of chronic dissatisfaction since the Soweto uprising. More than a thousand school yards either stood empty or were filled with the scenes of continuous disturbances as over a million students took up the cry, "Liberation Now! Education Later!" After the Vaal uprisings (November 1984), a massive two-day stay-away by 800,000 workers and 400,000 students also supported popular demands. The stay-away sent shivers through the business establishment, raising the specter of a general strike in South Africa's industrial heartland. It marked a historic convergence of interest between community organizations and the trade unions, which had previously preferred to stay aloof from overtly political action. The intensifying political struggles were drawing the workers' movement ever closer to the firing line.

In March 1985, even more successful stay-aways occurred in Port Elizabeth and Uitenhage in the eastern Cape. Supported by virtually all township residents, these actions signaled an intensification of the tactics employed in November as well as a regional shift in the focus of resistance. The eastern Cape became the new center of struggle. Here the consumer boycott was added to the armory of opposition. Angered by the compliance and even active support of business for the state in the intensifying conflict, community organizations decided to hit the business community where it hurt them most—in the pocket. The slogan "Business and government: flip sides of the same bloody coin of repression" summed up well the feeling behind these actions. The boycotts of white shops bankrupted many businesses and forced concessions from local authorities and the state; boycott leaders were released from detention so that an end to the boycott could be negotiated.

In the eastern Cape rural towns took part for the first time as the protest rapidly mushroomed into a national revolt. Small places that had been little more than dots on road maps—Port Alfred, Fort Beaufort, Queenstown, Graaff Reinet, and Cradock—became symbols of militancy.

Allister Sparks, seasoned correspondent for the *London Observer* and the *New York Times*, graphically described how the young militants (known as comrades) took the rebellion further in the eastern Cape than anywhere else.

The Port Elizabeth Youth Congress (PEYCO) effectively seized control of the Port Elizabeth townships and ran them as the closest thing South Africa has seen to "liberated zones." Official black councilors elected under the apartheid system were forced to resign or flee, black policemen took refuge in protected camps outside the townships, black youngsters walked out of the school in protest at what they termed "gutter education," and PEYCO street and area committees stepped into the vacuum. They issued trading licenses and fixed prices in black-owned shops; they policed the streets and set up "people's courts" to try common criminals as well as suspected criminal informers; and they talked about setting up "people's education" classes in garages and church halls.[7]

By mid-1985, resistance had deepened into open insurrection. The state, its reform program in tatters, was on the defensive. Following ANC strategy, the revolts were leading to "ungovernability" in the townships. The distinction between legal forms of politics and the underground struggle of the ANC was becoming blurred. Enthusiastic displays of support for the opposition groups occurred daily in open defiance of strict laws. Stirring *toyi-toyi* battle songs and dances—mimetic representations of armed struggle—came home to the townships from the guerrilla training camps. ANC flags and slogans appeared regularly at political occasions such as anniversaries of uprisings and at the newest form of political expression, the funeral service.

Unable to halt spreading disaffection in the townships, the government decided in July 1985 to proclaim a State of Emergency in thirty-six districts throughout the country. Virtual martial law descended over these areas. The government was acknowledging the collapse of reform, and its ever-increasing reliance on repression to maintain control.

By its standards, the government had exercised restraint until September 1984 because it wished to sell the reform package. True, it harassed activists, banned certain meetings, spread propaganda and misinformation, and on the eve of the elections in August 1984, detained more than twenty UDF leaders. But this was no more than "business as usual."

When the revolt broke out the following month, the state dropped all pretense of accommodation and tolerance. On the night of October 23, 1984, 7,000 soldiers and policemen cordoned off the Sebokeng township and carried out a door-to-door "anti-crime" operation in the middle of the night. A resident testified:

At about midnight I saw there were soldiers all over the street. . . . At about four o'clock they knocked on the door as if they wanted to kick it in. . . . Before they left they took a sticker and stuck it on a cupboard. It said, "Trust me, I am your friend. . . ."[8]

Similar operations followed in other townships. Soldiers fueled rather than calmed resistance. "Troops out" became a new addition to the list of anti-apartheid demands, but it soon became clear that the soldiers were in the townships to stay. The government acknowledged at the end of the year that some 32,000 troops had been deployed in ninety-six townships for the purpose of "preventing or suppressing internal disorder."

There were many allegations of atrocities by the police and army. A report prepared by the South African Catholic Bishops Conference stated that "the police are now regarded by many people in the black townships as disturbers of the peace and perpetrators of violent crime." Casualties rocketed as the siege of the townships spread. The number of deaths for 1985 alone was just under 800. On the twenty-fifth anniversary of the Sharpeville massacre on March 21, twenty people were shot dead by the police in an unprovoked attack at Langa near Uitenhage. This was the first of a number of mass killings that occurred during the year.

The state was rapidly closing existing avenues of legal protest and organization. In February 1985, the police raided UDF offices and the houses of more than 100 leading activists. All documents were confiscated. Meetings of the UDF and some of its affiliates were banned in eighteen magisterial districts. The state aimed to cripple and criminalize the UDF. A sustained state media propaganda campaign depicting the UDF as part of the communist-inspired onslaught on South Africa, prepared the ground for the crackdown.

More ominously, mysterious assassination and abduction squads began to appear. By early June, the UDF listed at least twenty-seven people missing and twelve victims of political assassination. Anti-apartheid activists were forced to go into hiding or flee the townships. These acts of terror were aimed precisely at those areas where resistance was strongest. The most chilling reminder of this new trend of naked extralegal terror came from the eastern Cape in July 1985, with the murders of Mathew Goniwe, a dynamic young leader who had risen to national prominence, and three UDF members. Their charred and horribly mutilated bodies were found several days after they were declared missing en route to Cradock after a meeting in Port Elizabeth.

Thirty thousand people from throughout South Africa streamed to the dusty little Karoo town for the funeral, which came to symbolize the whole spirit of mass resistance. For a day, Cradock was a liberated zone. Huge ANC flags were prominently displayed, and marshals dressed in ANC uniforms directed proceedings. In the white town nearby, streets were deserted and shutters drawn.

As the buses rolled out of the dusty township that night, P. W. Botha appeared on television to announce a State of Emergency. Unable to check the sweeping disaffection against apartheid, the state was now officially resorting to martial law. The emergency regulations gave the South African Defense Force (SADF) and police unrestrained powers, as well as virtual indemnity from prosecution. An 18-year-old national serviceman could use "whatever force he thinks is necessary" to stop anyone from "endangering public safety." Without a warrant or higher authorization, he could detain and imprison for fourteen days anyone he thought could endanger law and order, or search any person, vehicle, or premises and seize any article he believed could be used for any offenses. If the Minister of Law and Order thought they had acted in good faith, no one could bring criminal or civil proceedings against any member of the SADF, the police, or government. The commissioner of police was given far-reaching discretionary powers. He could impose curfews, control the publication of news relating to the State of Emergency or the conduct of the security forces, and place restrictions on funerals.

More than 10,000 people were detained during the first six months of emergency rule. For example, in the little town of Graaff Reinct, where resistance had been fierce, hundreds of people were rounded up and detained. Armed soldiers compelled schoolchildren to remain in the classroom between 8 A.M. and 2 P.M. Authorities closed black-owned shops to break the consumer boycott and force blacks back to the white business district. A curfew was enforced.

Emergency rule was accompanied by a dramatic increase in the extralegal terror noted earlier in the year. From Pieterburg in the north to Cape Town in the south, a stream of reports highlighted a new phenomenon. Bands of right-wing black vigilantes were on the move, intent on intimidating, injuring, and killing anti-apartheid activists, disrupting organizations, and overturning the balance of power held by anti-apartheid forces over the official pro-apartheid groups. In the urban areas, the vigilantes tended to have ties with community councilors, while in the rural Bantustans they often acted as paramilitary auxiliaries, waging war on opponents of the Bantustan structures. For example, in the KwaNdebele Bantustan "Prime Minister" Skosana reportedly supervised assaults on 400 abducted men in an area resisting incorporation into the Bantustan. In the KwaZulu Bantustan, a UDF member testified how a member of Parliament led a party that burned down his house and assaulted and shot his family as they tried to escape the fire. Many other brutal attacks on the democratic opposition took place in KwaZulu and in the adjoining South African province of Natal. They were usually linked to the amabutho ("the warriors"), marauding bands fired by Zulu chauvinism and frequently associated with the Inkatha movement of Chief Gatsha Buthelezi. After Inkatha had warned all UDF sympathizers to leave certain townships or face the consequences, rampaging impis armed with sticks and assegais (spears) were soon attempting to give meaning to this warning. The continuing clashes in Natal, which have cost hundreds of lives, had their genesis at this time.[9]

The rigors of martial law had failed to end mass resistance. Now the apartheid system was relying on the naked terror and violence of the vigilantes to destabilize and disrupt opposition. Vigilante terror was labeled "black-on-black" violence by the spokespersons of apartheid. To obscure the relationships between the conflicting parties and the apartheid structures, the government perpetuated racist stereotypes of tribal internecine warfare among blacks. By employing the old divide-and-rule tactic of attacking members of certain progressive organizations in the name of others, the system was also able to use vigilantes to divide its opponents, particularly AZAPO and the UDF.

Assault, arson, slashed or overinflated car tires, dead cats nailed to doors, bricks crashing through windows, bombed and burgled offices, and the ever present threat of death . . . these were the grim realities that anti-apartheid activists and organizations now had to face. And they could not count on the police for protection; indeed, there were widespread allegations of police complicity in these actions.[10]

The State of Emergency did not provide the solution envisaged by the apartheid state. Although seriously disrupted, militant resistance persisted within the country, and international opinion against apartheid reached new heights, leading to an increase in political and economic pressure from abroad and greater support for the anti-apartheid struggle.

All through the northern summer of 1985, as Newsweek noted, fiery images of the conflict in South Africa spilled across the world's television screens and front pages. Policemen clubbed and whipped defenseless protesters at prime time hours. The World Press Review rated South Africa high in the "top-ten" news items of the year. International pressure mounted as white politicians promised reform but delivered more repression. The South African economy went into a sharp downswing in the second half of 1985. The foreign exchange value of the rand plunged to its lowest point ever, necessitating the closure of the Johannesburg Stock Exchange for three days in order to stem the flow of capital out of the country. International corporations started withdrawing from South Africa. More than 100 corporations left as international disinvestment gathered momentum between 1985 and 1987. On the political front, the regime's international political allies—notably America's Ronald Reagan, Britain's Margaret Thatcher, and West Germany's Helmut Kohl—had hedged and stuck to so-called constructive engagement policies. Now they were forced to distance themselves from apartheid, agree to limited sanctions, and reassess their policies. The South African government, already an international outcast, was isolated as never before. As condemnation of the regime grew, so did the stature of its main antagonist, the banned ANC. For the first time, ANC President Tambo was received in Washington, London, and other capitals.

Internally, a pessimistic white community and business sector also started looking outside the laager for answers. In a single week, the Australian embassy received 1,700 applications from South Africans to emigrate. In September 1985, representatives of South African big business, which two years before had supported Botha's reform plans, flew to Lusaka for a historic meeting with the ANC.

Then, in January 1986, the leader of the official opposition resigned from Parliament, saying it had become ''irrelevant'' to those wishing to bring about genuine change in South Africa. Numerous other delegations representing a broad cross section of interests followed in the wake of the businessmen to meet with the ANC. The costs of apartheid were becoming so high that white South Africans started to look seriously to the ANC for the first time as an alternative for the future.

The ANC could claim without contradiction at this stage that ''the people are engaged in active struggle as a conscious revolutionary force and accept the ANC as their vanguard movement.'' At a historic conference held at Kabwe, Zambia, in mid-1985, the organization decided to step up its struggle from one of ''armed propaganda'' to full-scale ''people's war.'' The war was to be rooted in the townships, which were emerging ''perhaps in a rudimentary way'' as ''mass revolutionary bases.''[11] The various forms of struggle were to converge in a mass uprising. With its decision to escalate the struggle, the ANC was both responding to and shaping developments within South Africa.

Kabwe illustrated the strengthening of strategies and tactics of resistance in South Africa from mid-1985 onward. Buoyed by the success and intensity of the township revolts, the liberation groups started setting their eyes on the prize: state power. Faced by intense repression under the emergency, they reassessed their operations. A new rallying cry, ''From Ungovernability to People's Power,'' reflected the change in emphasis that occurred.

The government was unable to regain control in the townships, despite the State of Emergency. By the end of 1985, only a handful of the more than 100 local authorities the government had planned to set up were in existence. In their place, township residents were attempting to set up grass-roots street and area committees in order to organize residents on a street-to-street basis. This semi-underground system became so deeply embedded in certain areas that without even a pamphlet being issued a decision taken by the committees—a work stay-away, for instance—could be relayed, under the noses of the occupying forces, to an entire township, and adhered to by many thousands of people. Rent and consumer boycotts continued and spread countrywide, becoming a central resistance strategy. By August – September, no fewer than fifty-six centers were affected by rent boycotts and twenty-three by consumer boycotts. One consumer boycott, in Queenstown, lasted eight months.

Previously untouched areas of South Africa erupted in late 1985. In August, more than eighty people died in Durban, where rioting occurred after the assassination of a UDF leader, Victoria Mxenge, widow of a leader assassinated three years earlier. Police in Cape Town stopped marchers heading toward Pollsmoor Prison to demand the release of Nelson Mandela. In ensuing clashes, more than 100 people died, and the State of Emergency was extended to the western Cape. At the end of 1985, chronic disturbances spread to the rural Bantustans of Bophuthatswana, Lebowa, and KwaNdebele. Some areas became virtual ''no-go'' zones, and hundreds died as resistance continued. Every day there were reports of high

casualties: from Duncan Village, near East London—19 people dead, 138 injured; from Queenstown—14 killed after police broke up a meeting; from Mamelodi—13 shot during a peaceful march, some allegedly machine-gunned to death from a helicopter.

Mass funerals followed such events. Fifty thousand people turned up in Kwa Thema for the funeral of four of the seven young student activists slain by booby-trapped hand grenades after they had allegedly been approached by security force agents posing as ANC guerrillas. The same number of mourners came to Mamelodi. In East London, *Newsweek* estimated a crowd of 70,000. There were numerous smaller funerals. Police placed restrictions on the number who could attend funerals, and the routes to be followed. Often, mourners were tear-gassed, whipped, and dispersed—even killed. In one case, this writer witnessed security force helicopters clattering overhead at treetop level, drowning out prayers and hymns, as victims of police action were being laid to rest. A photograph in this book shows a police colonel trying to wrestle a banner from officiating ministers and mourners over the dead body of an ANC guerrilla.

When the township revolts first broke out in September 1984, the national resistance organizations had been caught off guard and had been unable to direct or control the spontaneous struggles. But by the end of 1985, the UDF had successfully made the transition from a front involved in anti-constitution protest politics to the cutting edge of an internal challenge to state power. The UDF gave coherence to the intensifying struggles throughout the country. Rent and consumer boycotts, the creation and maintenance of alternative structures, and other active campaigns increasingly assumed a more uniform character as the UDF adapted and grew in stature as a national organization.

COSATU soon joined the UDF in the work of national coordination. On November 30, 1985, the bulk of the country's independent trade unions combined to form the new national labor federation. COSATU brought together more than half a million workers, making it the biggest trade union grouping in the country. Through its thirty-three affiliates, COSATU reached into three and a half thousand workplaces and was represented by 12,000 elected shop stewards. Within a year, its membership had jumped to 750,000. The successful stay-aways in November 1984 and March 1985 laid the basis for an alliance between students, youth, and worker-parents. The unions now accepted that ''the struggle of the workers on the shop floor cannot be separated from the wider struggle for liberation.'' Within days of COSATU's formation, the general secretary traveled outside the country for consultation with the exiled ANC. COSATU declared that no solution could be found to the South African impasse ''without the full participation of the ANC, which is regarded by the majority of the people of South Africa as the overall leader and general representative.''

Early in 1986, the National Education Crisis Committee (NECC) was launched to coordinate action in the educational sphere. The NECC worked in unison with the trade unions and the political bodies, emphasizing clearly how the different strands of resistance were intersecting and giving shape to an increasingly coherent national struggle. Later, national youth and women's organizations—the South African Youth Congress and the Federation of South African Women—were formed. These rival black consciousness groupings were coordinating similar activities, though on a far smaller scale. In the local communities and at the national level, workers, students, unemployed youth, sports people, church members, and others were working together informally and through their organizations with a remarkable degree of common purpose. A grid of resistance, reaching throughout the country and into every sphere of struggle, was now in place.

A blinkered white community, kept cocooned from township realities by geographical segregation, government propaganda, and willful ignorance, put the "unrest" down to the work of a small minority of trouble-seeking agitators. But the uprisings undoubtedly enjoyed massive popular support. Behind each mass meeting, strike, township funeral, or street battle was a whole network of organization.

In a recent book on South Africa, Steven Davis froze a frame from typical newsreel footage of township rebellion to illustrate the political discipline and organization behind what appeared a confusing scene:

At first glance, the scene appears to be a ''standard'' riot: a maelstrom of police swinging batons and blacks hurling rocks. The same such encounter might have occurred decades ago. On closer inspection, however, differences emerge.

One of the dead on the street, his body burned by a gasoline-soaked tire ''necklace'' around his head, is a black suspected of having collaborated with the police. His killing was carried out by militants determined to blind the police by preventing access to intelligence information. On other occasions, impromptu ''people's courts'' in the townships investigate charges of complicity and mete out punishments. Behind the government troops is a row of factories, silent because their black workers have walked out in protest at the ''invasion'' of the township. Near the empty plants lie white-owned stores, where almost nothing is sold. Blacks are boycotting them to intensify pressure on white business to lobby against apartheid. Behind the protesters a building is smoldering. Molotov cocktails have gutted the government-run liquor concession that provides the official township authorities with revenue. Black-owned stores on the block remained untouched. In the distance, part of the township police station had been blown apart by a Soviet-manufactured limpet bomb planted late the previous night by a trained insurgent. Officers who man the station, together with the official township councilors and their families, have been forced to abandon their homes nearby for protection outside the community's borders.

The demonstration itself had been banned in advance by Pretoria, but thousands have turned out in defiance of the restriction at the behest of the unofficial civic organization, whose ''comrades'' have formed street committees throughout the township to mobilize residents. A few urban warriors, hiding in alleyways, aim AK-47s at the charging police. At the center of the melee young men and women are holding up two flags—the ANC's and the South African

Communist Party's. Underground members of the groups have smuggled the illegal banners to protesters. The materials may even have been purchased by ''taxes'' paid now by residents to the civic organization's ''comrades'' rather than to the government. Students have been excused from their newly ''liberated'' schools, which now feature anti-apartheid curricula designed by local militants to swell the demonstration as it collides with the wall of soldiers and armored vehicles. South African Defense Force units wait in the background for the call to reinforce beleaguered policemen. They are aware that in half a dozen locations throughout South Africa, similar confrontations are taking place at that very moment.[12]

What at first seemed a spontaneous riot is clearly far more significant. The violence in this paradigm skirmish is a consequence of a comprehensive and carefully assembled ''united front'' of opposition involving labor, consumers, civic organizations, schools and guerrilla action.

This composite portrait might have been drawn from the actual course of events in Alexandra, a township where struggle reached a peak of militancy and coordination. By early 1986, open war was waged on the streets. In February, more than twenty people died in nearly a week of clashes with police. Forty thousand people gathered to mourn the dead, and in the ensuing weeks the community took virtual control of the area. Councilors resigned one by one, policemen were forced to evacuate the area, and rent and consumer boycotts were imposed. In late April, after police had sealed off the township, mobs of balaclava-masked vigilantes blazed a trail of destruction through the area; eight anti-apartheid activists were killed and scores injured; sixty homes were firebombed and ten razed to the ground. Eyewitnesses maintained that the attacks took place under cover of police vehicles. As angry township residents retaliated, the newspaper headlines declared a ''township war zone.'' A crowd of 10,000 people marched fearlessly toward police, providing cover for gunmen whose AK-47s unloaded volley after volley at an estimated 100 policemen for nearly an hour. A journalist trapped in the cross fire gave a dramatic account:

Police moved forward with their guns cocked. The crowd kept coming. Then the crowd suddenly stopped and a salvo of gunfire sent the advancing police scattering. Policemen frantically took cover in little ditches and under the trees amid shouts of ''Dit is die AK . . . dis die AK.'' Police returned fire but the crowd stood as if they were glued to the road. One policeman tried to be brave and moved forward . . . gunfire rattled, and I heard the policeman yelling. It had caught him in the stomach. He moved back, his legs rubbery. . . . From my cramped position I could only see one of those firing from the crowd, a youngster of about 18, armed with an AK-47, who darted from one side of the road to the other, firing intermittent bursts.[13]

At an ensuing rally attended by 45,000 people, Alexandra residents resolved to form ''self-defense units'' to protect themselves. Residents dug ''tank traps'' in the dirt roads to prevent armored cars from entering. "Everyone seems to be involved as if it were some kind of community project," one witness reported. Early in May, as they waited the inevitable police and army onslaught, the community organizations declared that they were in "complete control of the area."

Such was the mood of militancy in 1986. In an attempt to regain the political initiative, the government lifted the State of Emergency and abolished the pass laws, which it could no longer effectively enforce. But this tactic only buoyed the opposition. May Day saw the biggest general strike in South African history. More than a million and a half workers obeyed a national stay-away call—and repeated this a few weeks later to commemorate the tenth anniversary of the Soweto uprisings on June 16.

The initiative clearly lay with the black masses. The ANC had effectively been "unbanned" by the people. Apartheid local government had collapsed. The regime had been forced to lift the State of Emergency and repeal the hated pass laws. Its reform program was in tatters. Internationally, it was isolated as never before. The economy was stuttering. The democratic forces were on the offensive. But, instead of a summer of people's power, a long hard winter of reaction lay ahead.

Living in the Interregnum: South Africa Today

The crisis consists precisely in the fact that the old is dying and the new cannot be born; in this interregnum a great variety of morbid symptoms appear.[14]

In mid-1986, after a decade and a half of increasing conflict and nearly two years of open rebellion, this scenario of an unresolved "organic" or structural crisis (painted by the Italian revolutionary Antonio Gramsci) applied aptly to South Africa. The country was in a state of violent equilibrium as the opposing forces of liberation and white minority rule locked horns. The former held the political initiative, enjoying mass support and legitimacy, but lacked the power to topple the state. The latter lacked legitimacy but controlled the levers of an advanced industrial economy and a strong state apparatus—including, crucially, loyal armed forces.

This situation greeted an international party of notables known as the Eminent Persons Group (EPG), representing the forty-nine Commonwealth nations, when it visited South Africa in an attempt to help break the political deadlock. Put simply, the EPG tried to persuade P. W. Botha to do what the majority of South Africans wanted him to do: hand over power to the ANC in the best interests of peace and the country's long-term stability.

They were rebuffed. Instead of discussing internationally supervised negotiations, P. W. Botha sent out SADF hit squads on missions against ANC targets in neighboring countries while the EPG mission was still in South Africa. A few weeks later, on the eve of the tenth anniversary of the 1976 Soweto uprising, Botha reimposed a State of Emergency and extended it from the previous thirty-

six "hot spots" to the entire country.

The South African government turned its back on international opinion and embarked on an all-out offensive to smash opposition to apartheid. It aimed to control the flow of information, smash mass organizations, restructure local politics, and restore stability by improving living conditions in the worst affected areas. If we must go it alone, so be it, declared Botha defiantly. New restrictions included tighter press gags and a wide-ranging prohibition on "subversive statements." Though there were thousands of detainees, newspapers were allowed to publish only those few named by the police. The police could regulate or prohibit "any comment or any news" relating to their conduct. Later, more curbs were added, such as the banning in certain areas of the publication of utterances of office bearers of more than 100 organizations. In an unintended tribute to George Orwell, the government set up a Bureau for Information whose daily press briefings were the only official source of news. Subsequently, all reports gathered by the local and international press had to be sanctioned by a new Inter-Departmental Press Liaison Center before they could be published. Several international reporters were forced to leave the country. Almost overnight the world lost sight of events in the South African townships. Behind this blanket of silence, the armored trucks moved in again. The state launched the most ferocious onslaught yet on democratic opposition. Within ten days of this new emergency, some 10,000 activists were rounded up; a year later, the figure had risen to about 30,000—equal to the total number held by the regime under security legislation and emergency rule in the twenty-six years since the Sharpeville era. The government acknowledged that at least 14,726 activists had been held longer than thirty days.

Among the detainees approximately 3,000 were women, and an estimated 10,000 were children of 17 years and under. Verbal accounts and affidavits by detainees, some reproduced in this book, related accounts of torture: electric shocks, beatings, and unprovoked shootings. An attorney whose clients included 11-year-olds examined "children whose wrists were bruised by handcuffs . . . children with lacerated tongues from electric wire pushed into their mouths during interrogations by the police . . .children with swollen eyes and gashed foreheads after they had been struck by rifle butts." In one incident she "accidentally" walked into a room in which children were being tortured:

I saw a group of 20 uniformed policemen, all carrying rifles, forcing a group of children to engage in very strenuous exercises. Some were crying, others were in shock, just blindly obeying. Another group of children, including five 11-year-olds, were squatting against the wall waiting for their turn. They were also closely guarded by police carrying very huge guns. Not pistols, but rifles.[15]

The plight of the children led to worldwide condemnation, and as a direct result the state banned the main detention monitoring group, the Detainees Parents Support Committee.

The widespread use of torture was verified by several independent studies, including one by a panel of doctors of the National Medical and Dental Association

(NAMDA) and another by the Institute of Criminology at the University of Cape Town, which found that more than 80 percent of detainees were tortured. During 1986, at least fifteen court actions were brought to restrain police from assaulting and torturing detainees. In a highly publicized case, a doctor employed in the district surgeon's office in Port Elizabeth corroborated the fact that torture was commonplace. The NAMDA report described over 600 cases, one fourth of which alleged sexual abuse. This usually consisted of people being stripped naked during interrogation and suffering assault on their sexual organs. One victim of such assault during interrogation was Father Smangaliso Mkatshwa, the secretary of the South African Catholic Bishops Conference. At least eighteen people detained for politically related reasons died in police custody between 1984 and 1986.

Besides detentions, the state continued with its usual methods of "formal repression": the continued security force siege of the townships, intense police surveillance, political trials, bannings, prohibition of meetings, listings, restrictions, deportations, and so forth. Activists were also subjected to "informal repression," including assassinations, attacks on homes and property, death threats, and bombed offices. The cumulative effect of these actions forced legal anti-apartheid activities underground.

The government accompanied its iron-fisted siege of the townships with a sophisticated new strategy. Almost imperceptibly, while detention swoops continued, armored vehicles and soldiers were being replaced by bulldozers and construction workers in many townships. "Street lights are being put up, trees planted, roads paved, drainage installed and sportsfields upgraded," read one report. The improvements, relegated to certain carefully selected townships described as "oil spots" (or "hot spots") were designed to lower the "revolutionary climate" and to separate anti-apartheid activists from the people with whom they had begun to develop the institutions of "people's power."

These operations, it now became clear, were being masterminded by the National Security Management System (NSMS), an elaborate structure of over 500 semi-secret committees dominated by the military and the police. As if by stealth, this shadowy structure which stretched from the president's office to every locality in the country had usurped many of the traditional functions of government, even at parliamentary and cabinet level. The "creeping military coup" was virtually complete.

The government hopes to achieve stability at the local level so that it can reinstate its shattered reform policy at the national level. To this end, the local "management committees" created under the NSMS set out to restructure from the bottom up by improving local conditions, strengthening government collaborators, and ensuring that anti-apartheid activity is disrupted. A prominent lawyer noted how the management councils "sit there and work out how to take a community apart by detaining activists [and uprooting the whole support network of organizations, advice offices, crèches, resource centers, and newspapers] and reconstituting it without them. They are then released one by one into a vacuum."[16] At the same time, the state tried to strengthen the hand of local collaboraters by rushing

thousands of hastily recruited *kitskonstabels* (literally "instant constables") through a six-week training course and sending them into the townships as local police. Their sole purpose was to "keep order." People claimed that the armed vigilantes of 1985 had become the uniformed constables of 1986.

The ruthless way in which the state moved to restructure local politics was nowhere better illustrated than in the "hot spots" of Alexandra, Crossroads, and Kwanobuhle, which had been beacons of resistance. In Alexandra, a 100 million rand upgrade operation swung into gear as the state prepared to charge Moses Mayekiso and other Alexandra community leaders with treason. New schools were being built, and thousands of township children were being bused into white areas for cricket coaching in a hearts-and-minds campaign. In Langa, the entire population of 40,000 was moved against their wishes to a new location away from "white" Uitenhage, the nearest town. Similar mass evictions occurred at the Crossroads squatter camp where a month of fighting between state-backed armed vigilantes and "comrades" left sixty people dead and over 70,000 homeless. Numerous witnesses testified in court and outside how the stalemated battle swung against the latter after police had "laid a carpet of tear gas" and advanced into the area, putting the "comrades" (and residents defending their homes) to flight, before standing aside so that the vigilantes could overrun and torch the area. A refuge center and some 5,000 shacks were burnt. Police and army cordoned off the area with barbed wire and refused to let the inhabitants return. The state insisted that they move to another area twenty kilometers away. Then, having cleared the area of people, property, and "politics," it put into operation a multimillion rand "upgrade" scheme in collaboration with its allies—satisfied that it had eliminated yet another "hotbed" of resistance.

The State of Emergency clearly fulfilled its immediate objective of containing the open rebellion that had raged in the black townships between September 1984 and May 1986. By mid-1987, police reported that violent incidents had dropped by 80 percent. The government had won a battle, but certainly not the war: it was further than ever from the political settlement that it knows is crucial for peace. The opposition refused to lie down.

On the first anniversary of the June 1986 State of Emergency, UDF Secretary Murphy Morobe reminisced about the lively forms of mass protest—the rallies, public funerals, marches, and street protests—that had characterized resistance before the emergency, saying, "Those days have passed." Morobe had emerged from almost a year in hiding to give a press interview, causing one reporter to observe the irony that Morobe had become "a public relations man who cannot be seen in public, representing a legal mass organization that has to operate underground."

Despite the changed situation, the UDF and other organizations refused to give up their roles as legal organizations committed to nonviolent action. This was important, Morobe explained, because "the state is trying to move us from an area [the open political arena] where we have been able to strike significant blows against apartheid and move us to a sphere where it believes it is stronger—the area of violence.'' The state moved in this direction because it had no answers and lacked legitimacy. The UDF challenged the emergency in the courts, but, typically, the government's response was to redraft regulations proved invalid and to introduce new curbs. It was constantly moving the goal posts. In February 1988, the government suspended the charade of democracy altogether. It prohibited seventeen of the major organizations in the country, including the UDF, ''from carrying on, or performing, any acts whatsoever.'' When the churches (one of the few remaining avenues of expression) protested near Parliament, church leaders, including Archbishop Desmond Tutu, were arrested. As of the writing of this article, therefore, all effective opposition to apartheid has been outlawed.

The effect of government repression has been twofold. On the one hand, it has driven open anti-apartheid activities underground, and on the other, it has generated new strategies and forms of resistance. An important consequence has been the shift of the trade unions into the center of the political stage. In 1987, COSATU adopted the Freedom Charter as its guiding document, thereby formally aligning itself with the ANC, the UDF, and other forces in the Charterist camp. ''The interests of the working class can only be advanced by us locating ourselves in the hub of the struggle. . .,''[18] explained COSATU General Secretary Jay Naidoo.

The total number of strikes in 1987 was eight times higher than in 1986, the previous annual record. Repression inevitably followed. During April 1987, a six-week strike by South African Transport Services workers cost the state millions of rand. Authorities dismissed all 16,000 striking workers. Eight workers were shot, and the state forces laid siege to the national headquarters of COSATU for more than eight hours. A photograph in this book dramatically documents the scene recounted by a union official:

> As night fell, COSATU House was in a state of siege. Our building was stormed, and the security forces moved systematically through each floor assaulting people indiscriminately, breaking down office doors, and vandalizing our union property. The police and army . . . withdrew, detaining hundreds and leaving in their wake a trail of blood and damage.[19]

''Bloody Wednesday'' was a signal from the regime that the onslaught had started. The state-run television corporation churned out anti-COSATU propaganda, and a few weeks later a huge bomb explosion ripped through COSATU House, destroying the union's printing works and causing heavy damage. Government inspectors subsequently declared the eight-story building unsafe, and COSATU was compelled to evacuate it. A similar explosion occurred at the regional headquarters in Cape Town, and there followed a series of arson attacks and vandalism on union property throughout the country. Offices were closed, and unionists went into hiding.

Later in 1987, COSATU's biggest affiliate, the National Union of Mineworkers, took on the mining houses for three and a half weeks in a strike involving more than a quarter of a million workers. Clearly, the political struggle was shifting into the industrial sphere. In the February 1988 clampdown, the government barred COSATU from ''political activities,'' and it later amended the Labor Relations Act to further hamstring unions and curtail the right to strike.

While political organizations and the labor movement bore the brunt of the systematic onslaught of the state, the past two years have also revealed ''a national pattern whereby remaining enclaves of legally constituted anti-apartheid organizations [in the universities, the press, the churches, and elsewhere] are being destroyed, one by one.'' This destruction is being achieved through official actions and terror campaigns waged by elements operating outside the ''legal'' boundaries of emergency and security legislation. A bill aimed at monitoring and stifling any dissent on university campuses was withdrawn only after the court agreed with the universities that the regulations were so vague and loosely worded that they could not be implemented. In 1988 and 1989, a number of newspapers were temporarily banned as a result of new media restrictions. More ominously, in a year that saw the churches adopt an increasingly aggressive political posture to help fill the vacuum created by the bans on political activity, the multistoried headquarters of the South African Council of Churches was destroyed in a massive bomb blast in August 1988. This was at least the fourteenth case of bombing or arson on anti-apartheid organizations since the almost identical bombing of COSATU's headquarters the previous year.

The state's latest onslaught may have thrown the anti-apartheid struggle into some disarray, but it has not rooted out or destroyed the massive legitimacy the movement enjoys. Unlike the Sharpeville era in the early 1960s, the struggles of the past few years have been too widespread and too deeply rooted to be consigned to memory. Two massive stay-aways in March and June 1988 drove home the point. These actions were illegal under both the emergency regulations and the February restrictions. No public calls could be made, no organization set up. Yet millions of workers stayed away. The June stay-away lasted three days and was the biggest mass demonstration in South African history. It showed unambiguously that opposition to the South African government and its policies remains intense despite the government's repression and claims to the contrary.

Each move by a repressive state to impose an artificial calm in South Africa meets with new strategies and forms of opposition that place the central non-negotiable issue of economic justice and full political rights for all South Africans firmly back on the political agenda. The government knows that it cannot avoid these issues, but it has no answer except force. The Minister of Law and Order has admitted, ''We will have to find a political solution acceptable to the majority—otherwise we will lose.''[20]

The government hoped that the local elections in October 1988 would win enough support for it to relaunch the reform program, but the great majority of township residents again boycotted. Nationally, the government wants to set up an advisory National Statutory Council to accommodate black aspirations, but there have been no takers because this package also comes in the old apartheid wrapping. The government holds out the prospect of releasing Nelson Mandela (who it cannot incarcerate forever), but shows no sign that it will take the next step of negotiating with Mandela and other black leaders. Its inability to break the political impasse was well illustrated by the release from Robben Island of Mandela's colleague, Govan Mbeki. He left prison after twenty-five years reaffirming his loyalty to the ANC and was received with tremendous enthusiasm. The security police expected 100,000 people at a welcoming rally. The response of the government was typical. Having raised expectations that it might talk to Mbeki, it banned all rallies, refused permission for him to be quoted, and restricted him to his home area instead. For the "father of the struggle," one form of imprisonment replaced another, the same treatment that Nelson Mandela can expect when he is released.

This event highlighted the dilemma of the apartheid regime. By its own admission the solution to the crisis in the country is 80 percent political and 20 percent military. However, its repressive actions show an inverse application of the formula. The regime knows it must talk, but it does not like what it hears, and so wields the big stick. This reaction serves only to fuel resentment. The Nationalists rule, but not with consent. Unable to meet the political aspirations of the black majority, the government resorts increasingly to naked force. And, as South Africa journeys on through the interregnum, a great variety of morbid symptoms appear.

Notes

1. *Weekly Mail,* August 28, 1987; *Cape Times,* September 18, 1987.

2. "Strategy and Tactics of the ANC," Morogoro, 1969 in *ANC Speaks: Documents and Statements of the African National Congress,* p. 173.

3. See Mike Savage, "The Costs of Apartheid," *Third World Quarterly,* vol. 9, no. 2, April 1987, pp. 601–621.

4. Quoted in Colin Bundy, "South Africa on Switchback," *New Society,* January 3, 1986, pp. 7–12.

5. Frederick van Zyl Slabbert, "The Dynamics of Reform and Revolt in South Africa," *IDASA Occasional Papers,* no. 8, 1987, p. 3.

6. Herman Giliomee, *The Parting of the Ways: South African Politics, 1976–1982* (Cape Town, 1982), p. xi.

7. A. Sparks, "The Emergency . . . One Year Older," *Sunday Tribune,* June 7, 1987 (in *SA Press Clips Supplement,* Cape Town, 1987).

8. Quoted in South African Catholic Bishops Conference report, "Police Conduct During the Township Protests: August-November 1984" (Pretoria, 1985).

9. See Nicholas Haysom, *Mabangalala: The Rise of Right-wing Vigilantes in South Africa* (Johannesburg, 1986).

10. See, for example, *Weekly Mail,* May 20, 1988.

11. Documents of the Second National Consultive Conference on the African National Congress, Zambia, June 16–23, 1985, p. 34.

12. Steven M. Davis, *Apartheid's Rebels: Inside South Africa's Hidden War* (New Haven, 1987), pp. 77–78.

13. *Cape Times,* April 24, 1986.

14. Quoted in Mark Swilling, "Living in the Interregnum: Crisis, Reform and the Socialist Alternative in South Africa," *Third World Quarterly,* vol. 9, no. 2, April 1987, p. 408.

15. *IDAF Focus,* no. 75, March–April 1988.

16. Phillip van Niekerk, "At Five to Midnight They Came in Three Columns," *Die Suid Afrikaan,* no. 11, September 1987, p. 35.

17. *Weekly Mail,* June 12, 1987.

18. Glen Moss and Ingrid Obery (eds.), *South African Review,* vol. 4 (Johannesburg, 1988), p. 247.

19. Ibid, p. 233.

20. *Cape Times,* November 30, 1987.

There is not the space here to acknowledge all the sources that have been used in this article. The most important ones, however, are listed below. The purpose is to guide the reader who wishes to venture further than the article can go, and to acknowledge the writer's debt to the works mentioned. In several cases I borrowed heavily from them. On the structural crisis facing apartheid and the "reform" program this has engendered, see Catholic Institute for International Relations (CIIR), *South Africa in the 1980s: State of Emergency* (London, 1986); Philip Frankel, Noam Pines, and Mark Swilling, eds., *State, Resistance, and Change in South Africa* (London, 1988); Hermann Giliomee, *The Parting of the Ways: South African Politics, 1976–1982.* (Cape Town, 1982); John Saul and Stephen Gelb, *The Crisis in South Africa: Class Defense, Class Revolution* (New York, 1981); and Frederick van Zyl Slabbert, "The Dynamics of Reform and Revolt in South Africa," *IDASA Occasional Papers,* nos. 7–9, 1987. For a background to the struggle against apartheid in South Africa, see Rob Davies, Dan O'Meara, and Sipho Dlamini, *The Struggle for South Africa: A Reference Guide to Movements, Organisations and Institutions* (London, 1984). For information on the resurgence of resistance since 1983, see William Cobbet and Robin Cohen, eds., *Popular Struggles in South Africa* (London, 1988); Steven M. Davis, *Apartheid's Rebels: Inside South Africa's Hidden War* (New Haven, 1987); the above-mentioned study by Frankel, Pines, and Swilling (as well as the latter's recent articles); Martin Murray, *South Africa: Time of Agony, Time of Destiny—The Upsurge of Popular Protest* (London, 1987); and *South African Review,* vols. 3–4. The *Weekly Mail, New Nation, Work In Progress,* and *South African Labour Bulletin* provide excellent coverage of the struggle and the debates occurring within it. The annual *Survey of Race Relations,* published by the South African Institute of Race Relations, and the press clippings service run by Barry Streek in Cape Town are valuable sources of information. Internationally, an excellent information service on South Africa is provided by the International Defense and Aid Fund for Southern Africa (IDAF), which publishes regular briefing papers, pamphlets, and books on a wide variety of topics.

Many people have helped in one way or another with this work. I am grateful to them all. I especially want to thank Paul Weinberg, Andrew Boraine, and Omar Badsha for their initial help, Mike Kirkwood for his editorial advice, and Liz Offen for her constant support and encouragement.

ACKNOWLEDGMENTS

Work on *Beyond the Barricades* has gone forward under extraordinarily difficult circumstances because of the lack of freedom of speech and freedom of the Press in South Africa. As a result, the editors and designer have, ultimately, made all decisions about the photographs and the placement of the texts. The editors take full responsibility for the writing and selecting of all textual materials. Any errors or doubtful interpretations are unintentional, but the responsibility is ours. We want to thank Lesley Lawson, who researched and collected in South Africa a large number of affidavits and other texts, and Michael Kirkwood, who from his home in England provided the initial material for the captions. In thanking Omar Badsha, Gideon Mendel, and Paul Weinberg for selecting a powerful and informative set of photographs, we wish to say that this book is built around images that speak in ways words cannot. In bringing this varied and complicated body of material into book form, we want especially to acknowledge the work of Margaret Sartor. Although credited as the designer, she has been more than that and has helped to shape this book conceptually as well as visually.

In preparing *Beyond the Barricades* for publication the editors have also relied on the help and advice of people whose knowledge about South Africa far exceeds our own. We would like to thank Laura Mangan for her thorough review of the captions and texts and for the difficult-to-obtain information she provided from her personal files on South Africa. Geoff Sifrin befriended the project from the beginning and guided us to others who could help us complete the research for the book. At Duke University Sheridan Johns in the Political Science Department and Lawrence Baxter in the Law School offered help with finding sources that were difficult to locate in the U.S. Allister Sparks, who was, to our good fortune, a visiting journalist at Duke, gave us the benefit of his extraordinary wisdom about his troubled country. Throughout, we have been grateful for the astute advice and keen eye of Steve Dietz at Aperture and for his support in completing this project.

Iris Tillman Hill and Alex Harris
Durham, North Carolina

We wish to thank all those South Africans, both at home and in exile, who have assisted us in making this book possible. To Graham Goodard, a special thanks for undertaking the monumental task of printing ten copies of the exhibition. We are grateful to that courageous and brave South African, Frank Chikane, for generously giving his time in writing the foreword for this book. To the photographers, for their contribution and commitment to this project and for their support in helping us to develop an alternative way of seeing and exhibiting. Also to Alex Harris and Margaret Sartor of the Center for Documentary Studies at Duke University for the hard work and dedication that they have put into supporting the efforts of documentary photographers in South Africa. We are grateful to Iris Tillman Hill of the Center for Documentary Studies for her fine work and long hours on this project, without which this book would not have been possible. Thanks also to the Comite Catholique contre la Faim et pour le Developpement (CCFD, France) for their assistance in making this book and exhibitions possible. Thanks to Mike Kirkwood for assisting with the editing and acting as editorial advisor. Finally we thank our publishers with whom we share the vision of a new society.

Omar Badsha, Gideon Mendel, and Paul Weinberg
Cape Town and Johannesburg

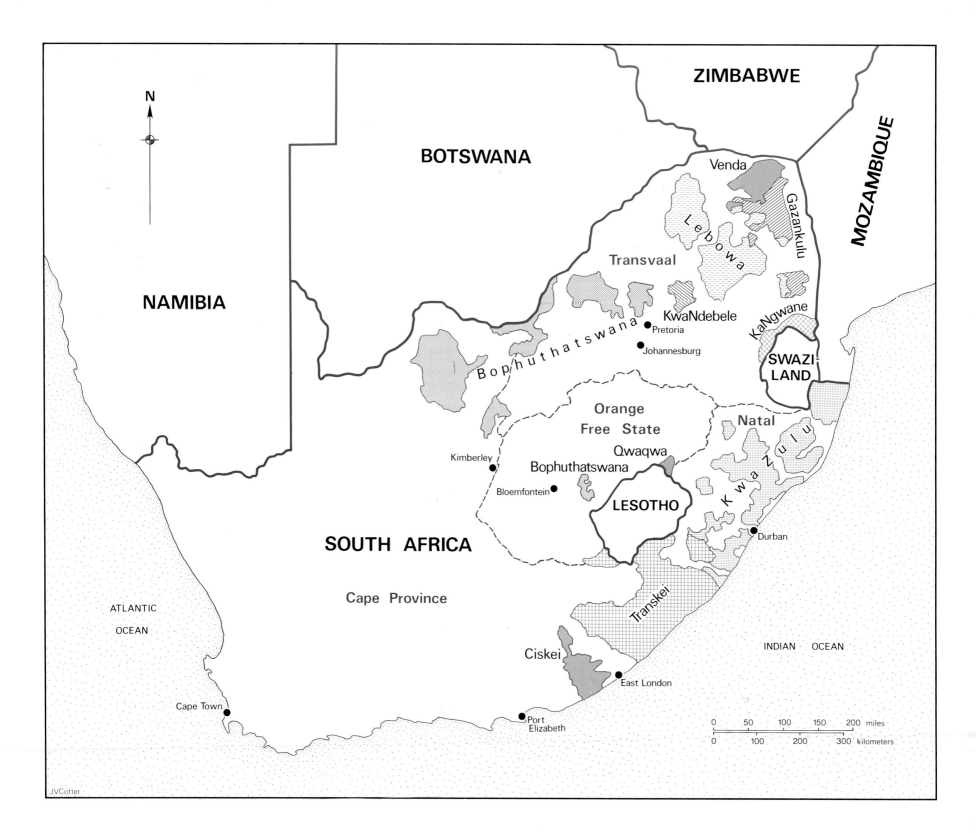

ZIMBABWE

MOZAMBIQUE

N

BOTSWANA

NAMIBIA

Venda

Gazankulu

Lebowa

Transvaal

KwaNdebele

● Pretoria

● Johannesburg

Bophuthatswana

KaNgwane

SWAZI-
LAND

Orange
Free State

Natal

Qwaqwa

Kimberley ●

Bophuthatswana

K w a z u l u

Bloemfontein ●

LESOTHO

● Durban

SOUTH AFRICA

ATLANTIC
OCEAN

Cape Province

Transkei

INDIAN OCEAN

Ciskei

● East London

● Cape Town

● Port
Elizabeth

0   50   100   150   200 miles

0   100   200   300 kilometers

JVCotter

140

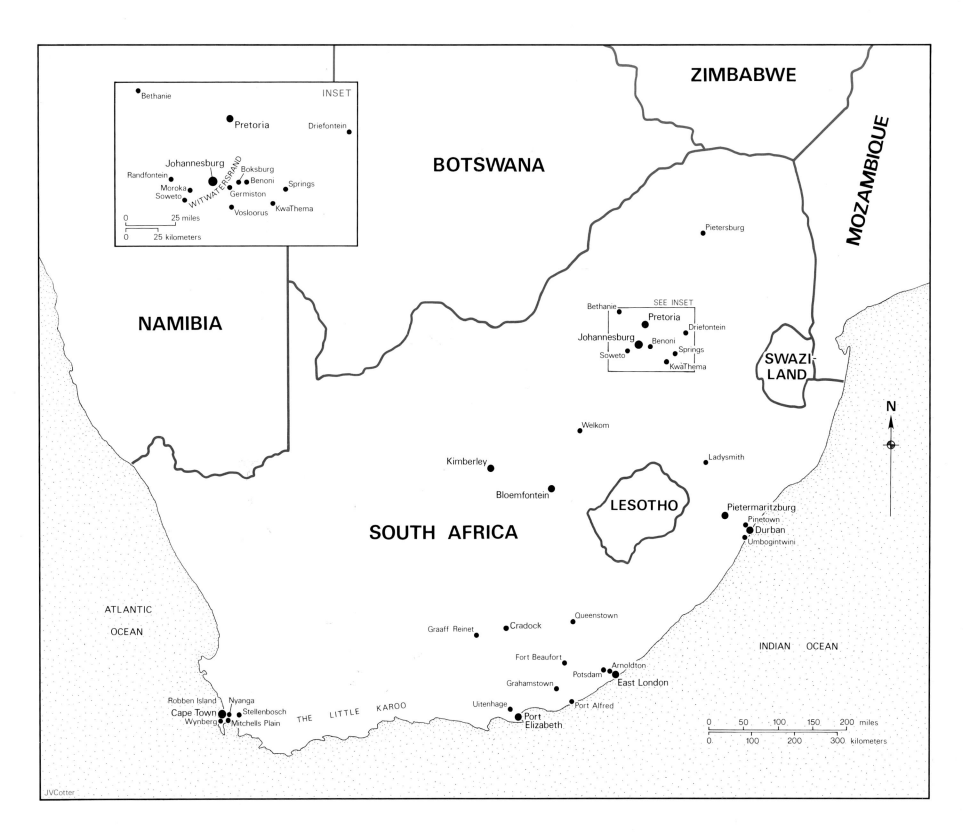

INSET

Bethanie

Pretoria

Driefontein

Johannesburg

WITWATERSRAND

Randfontein

Boksburg

Benoni

Moroka

Springs

Soweto

Germiston

KwaThema

Vosloorus

0   25 miles

0   25 kilometers

ZIMBABWE

MOZAMBIQUE

BOTSWANA

NAMIBIA

Pietersburg

SEE INSET

Bethanie

Pretoria

Johannesburg

Driefontein

Benoni

Soweto

Springs

KwaThema

SWAZI-
LAND

Welkom

Kimberley

Ladysmith

Bloemfontein

LESOTHO

Pietermaritzburg

Pinetown

Durban

Umbogintwini

SOUTH AFRICA

ATLANTIC

OCEAN

N

INDIAN   OCEAN

Queenstown

Graaff Reinet

Cradock

Fort Beaufort

Arnoldton

Potsdam

East London

Grahamstown

Robben Island

Nyanga

Uitenhage

Port Alfred

Cape Town

Stellenbosch

THE   LITTLE   KAROO

Port
Elizabeth

Wynberg

Mitchells Plain

0   50   100   150   200 miles

0   100   200   300 kilometers

JVCotter

141

PHOTOGRAPHIC CREDITS

Omar Badsha pp. 16, 17, 20, 25, 26 (*top*), 26 (*middle*), 30 (*bottom*), 36, 39, 60, 65, 104, 106, 108, 109, 115

Julian Cobbing pp. 51, 75, 89

Paul Grendon p. 97

Steve Hilton-Barber pp. 48, 83 (*top*), 92

Dave Hartman pp. 33, 80, 91, 95

Rashid Lombard p. 37

Roger Meintjies pp. 94, 117

Gideon Mendel pp. 12, 27, 31, 41, 43, 52, 53, 74, 77, 85, 93, 98, 99

Eric Miller pp. 102, 103, 105

Santu Mofokeng p. 84

Themba Nkosi p. 49

Cedric Nunn pp. 15, 57, 73

Billy Paddock pp. 66, 68, 82

Myron Peters p. 30 (*top*)

Chris Qwazi p. 90

Jeeva Rajgopaul p. 112

Guy Tillim pp. 11, 67, 70

Zubeida Vallie p. 83 (*bottom*)

Gill de Vlieg p. 18, 54, 55, 81

Paul Weinberg pp. 13, 14, 19, 21, 26 (*bottom*), 34, 35, 38, 56, 59, 61, 71, 107, 113

LIST OF SOURCES

List of sources for the texts in order of their appearance:

"Today," by Nise Malange, *Black Mamba Rising: South African Worker Poets in Struggle* (Worker Resistance and Culture Publications, 1986), p. 64.

"Freedom Song," *South Africa: A Different Kind of War,* edited by Julie Frederickse (Johannesburg: Ravan Press, 1986), p. 184.

"They Would Follow Her," "The Children Suffer Most," "We Are Sick and Tired," *Vukani Makhosikazi: South African Women Speak,* edited by Jane Barrett, et al. (London: Catholic Institute for International Relations, 1985), pp. 122, 236, 252.

"We Decided to Burn Our Passes," from "The General of Cradock," *Learn and Teach,* no. 3, 1986, pp. 31–33.

"The Houses Are Cracked and Broken," *Vukani Makhosikazi: South African Women Speak,* edited by Jane Barrett, et al. (London: Catholic Institute for International Relations, 1985), pp. 254–256.

"We Want All Our Rights," *South Africa: A Different Kind of War,* edited by Julie Frederickse (Johannesburg: Ravan Press, 1986), p. 150.

"Tambo's voice is heard calling," "How do I tell this long tale?" excerpts from *A Tough Tale,* a poem by Mongane Serote (London: Kliptown Books, 1987), pp. 28, 31.

"My Mother," by Chris van Wyk, *Ten Years of Staffrider Magazine* (Johannesburg: Ravan Press, 1988), p. 187.

"We Are Becoming Dangerous," *South Africa: A Different Kind of War,* edited by Julie Frederickse (Johannesburg: Ravan Press, 1986), p. 184.

"Why Are You Taking My Mother?" *Die Trojaanse Perd,* edited by Hans Pienaar and Hein Willemse (Taurus, n.d.), pp. 68–69.

"There Were Many of Us in the Cell," *Vukani Makhosikazi: South African Women Speak,* edited by Jane Barrett, et al. (London: Catholic Institute for International Relations, 1985), pp. 260–261.

"We Have Always Been Scared," "They Just Started Beating Her," "I Lost Consciousness," *Now Everyone Is Afraid: The Changing Face of Policing in South Africa* (London: Catholic Institute for International Relations, August 1988), pp. 50–61.

"I Was Then Hit, Whipped, and Sjambokked," from a signed affidavit, in *A.K.T. and Others, Applicant, and the Minister of Law and Order and Others, Respondent,* 16 August 1986, the Supreme Court of South Africa (Orange Free State Division), from the files of the Legal Resources Centre, Cape Town.

"Shoot, You Have Already Shot My Son," in "A Case Study: Jansenville—Divide and Rule," *Greenflies: Municipal Police in the Eastern Cape,* a published document, Black Sash, 1988.

"I Was Terrified," from a signed affidavit, 20 November 1985, Black Sash.

"The Children Are Not Scared of Death," *Vukani Makhosikazi: South African Women Speak,* edited by Jane Barrett, et al. (London: Catholic Institute for International Relations, 1985), p. 232.

"This Poem Is Dedicated to Brother Andries Raditsela," by Nise Malange, *Black Mamba Rising: South African Worker Poets in Struggle* (Worker Resistance and Culture Publications, 1986), p. 63.

"Why Did God Create a Human Being?" *Two Dogs and Freedom: Children of the Townships Speak Out* (Johannesburg: The Open School/Ravan Press, and New York: Rosset & Co., 1986).

"They Handcuffed Me and Chained Me," "The Tear Gas Was Too Much," from signed affidavits, *Memorandum on the Suffering of Children in South Africa,* Black Sash, April 1986.

"Some of Us Fainted," from "Statements Taken in Bhongolethu," *The Last Affidavits* (South African Catholic Bishops Conference, 1987), pp. 27–28.

"I Heard Loud Knocking," a signed affidavit from the Pietermaritzburg district, in the files of Cheadle, Thompson, and Haysom, attorneys.

"We learnt from the pain and sorrow," "School children took to the street," excerpts from "Time Has Run Out," a poem by Mongane Serote, *Ten Years of Staffrider Magazine* (Johannesburg: Ravan Press, 1988), p. 225.

"Within a month the 'sensitive situation' had become a bloody one," "Vigilantes," "They Wanted to Kill Me," "I Asked for Mercy," "I Fear for My Life," "The House was Burning," *Mabangalala: The Rise of Right Wing Vigilantes in South Africa,* by Nicholas Haysom (Johannesburg: University of Witwatersrand, Centre for Applied Legal Studies, Occasional Paper no. 10), pp. 2, 38–93.

"The Police Are There," "I Observed the Fighting," from signed affidavits, in *Mbewana and Others* v. *The Minister of Law and Order,* case no. 5317-86, Cape Provincial Division of the Supreme Court, court records on the Crossroads/KTC conflict, provided by Cape Town Legal Resources Centre.

"The souls of those killed cry out," from a funeral speech by Bishop Tutu, Raleigh (N.C.) *News and Observer,* 1 September 1986.

"He Was Beaten to Death," from an affidavit, "Deaths in Custody: Seven Recent Cases," Lawyers for Human Rights, July 1986, Legal Resources Centre's files, Cape Town, no. 315.

"Quite a Handful Disappeared without a Trace," from "A Short Background to Shooting Incident in Langa Township, Uitenhage," T. T. Majodina, an unpublished document in the Legal Resources Centre's files, Cape Town, no. 211.

"Inquests into the Deaths of M. C. Miranda and S. Magmost and J. Classen before Magistrate Mr. G. Hollman, held at Wynberg, December 1987," from court records (inquest nos. 493, 494, 495/78/88), provided by Legal Resources Centre, Cape Town.

"The Service Could Continue and Stop as Soon as Possible," a statement about the funeral service for the late Mandlenkosi Tokwe at Joza Stadium on 13 April 1986, from the Black Sash Archives.

"We Had Just Buried Our Children," an anonymous testimony describing the "Alex War" of February 1986, *Learn and Teach,* no. 2, 1986.

"We Would Win Because We Were United," from "The O.K. Strike: A Long and Hard Struggle," *Learn and Teach*, no. 2, 1987, pp. 9–12.

"I Was Earning a Lower Wage than That Dress," *Working Woman* (Johannesburg: Sached/Ravan Press, 1985), p. 67.

"You Find These Men by the Smell," *Learn and Teach*, no. 3, 1983, p. 2.

"The Story of One Tells the Struggle of All," *The Sun Shall Rise for the Workers*, by Mandlenkosi Makhoba (Johannesburg: Ravan Press, Ravan Workers Series, 1984), pp. 2, 3, 15, 19.

"A Sermon by a Local Parish Priest," Matola Commemoration Service at Regina Mundi Church, Soweto, 22 February 1981, *South Africa: A Different Kind of War*, edited by Julie Frederickse (Johannesburg: Ravan Press, 1986).

"Security Emergency Regulations," *Government Gazette of the Republic of South Africa*, vol. 276, no. 11340, pp. 2–6; no. 11341, pp. 2–3; no. 11342, pp. 4–10, no. 11343, p. 2; no. 11344, pp. 1–4.

"Who Are They?" by Walt oyiSipho ka Mtetwa, *Staffrider*, vol. 6, no. 2, 1985, p. 48.

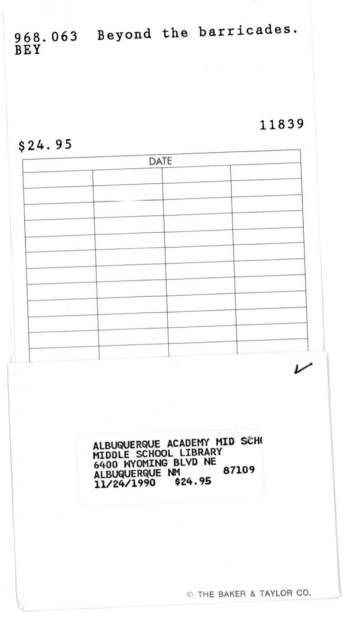